Unity a

A National Conversation

BARTON LECTURES

EDITED BY HELEN IRVING

Unity and Diversity:
A National Conversation

Barton Lectures

Edited by Helen Irving

Published by ABC Books for the
AUSTRALIAN BROADCASTING CORPORATION
GPO Box 9994 Sydney NSW 2001

Copyright © in this collection, Australian Broadcasting Corporation 2001

Copyright © in individual lectures remains with the lecturers

First published November 2001

All rights reserved. No part of this publication
may be reproduced, stored in a retrieval system
or transmitted in any form or by any means,
electronic, mechanical, photocopying, recording
or otherwise, without the prior written permission
of the Australian Broadcasting Corporation.

National Library of Australia
Cataloguing-in-Publication entry
Unity and diversity : the Barton Lectures 2001.
 ISBN 0 7333 1031 1.
 1. Pluralism (Social sciences). 2. Australia - Social conditions.
 3. Australia - Social life and customs. I. Irving, Helen.
 II. Australian Broadcasting Corporation.
306.0994

Designed by Helen Semmler
Cover design by Reno Design
NSW Centenary of Federation Committee
Set in 10.5/15 pt Garth Graphic by
Midland Typesetters, Maryborough, Victoria
Colour separations by Colorwize, Adelaide
Printed and bound in Australia by
Griffin Press, Adelaide

5 4 3 2 1

FOREWORD

Contributing to the national conversation

In 2001, Australia marked the centenary of the creation of the Commonwealth through the federation of the six previously separate colonies. National and state centenary bodies had been set up to plan an Australian approach to what would be an event-filled year. This was more than just an opportunity for a party. The centenary of Federation invited reflection on both the historical decision to federate and on the evolution of the Commonwealth over its hundred years of life. Even those who might otherwise have been indifferent could agree that the exchange of ideas about the significance of these events had potential for a lasting contribution, transcending mere celebration.

The New South Wales Centenary of Federation Committee was established in 1997 with the premier, the Hon. Bob Carr as president, and former premier the Hon Barrie Unsworth as chair. Premier Carr then extended an invitation to Professor Donald Horne, one of Australia's best-known public intellectuals, to lead and contribute to the centenary planning. When Professor Horne, as a member of the NSW Centenary of Federation Committee proposed among other things that there should be a series of lectures addressing the major questions confronting Australia in 2001, his idea was adopted with enthusiasm.

A series of ten public lectures was conceived and named in honour of the leading New South Wales federalist and first Australian prime minister Edmund Barton. Ten Australians, representing a range of views and backgrounds, were invited to speak about the different forms of diversity and the sources of unity that have shaped, and continue to shape, Australian society. The changes and continuities experienced by Australians in class, gender, ethnicity, and cultural and constitutional relations became the focus of individual lectures.

Organised by Mary Gray, the NSW Centenary of Federation Manager in Education History and Civics and Anna Roache the Manager of International and State Programs, the Barton Lectures were delivered between February and April 2001 to enthusiastic audiences in hostorically relevant venues in Sydney and regional New South Wales. Edited extracts were published in the *Australian* and the full lectures, including audience participation, were broadcast on ABC Radio National.

Federation was itself a great and persistent idea, one that ultimately stirred the public imagination in the 1890s and inspired Australians to take an unprecedented leap into a new way of thinking about themselves. It created a whole new layer of politics and a new set of constitutional practices. It gave rise to a designed national capital, Canberra, as well as many great national institutions. For one hundred years the Commonwealth has functioned, grown and evolved. The Australian people have also changed and redefined themselves, evolving from a settler population of predominantly British origin into a multicultural and diverse nation-state, one in which the Aboriginal inhabitants are beginning to be acknowledged and the importance of Australia's regional associations with Asia is openly debated. Our century has witnessed a continuing exchange and dialogue between the enduring and the shifting, between what is unique to Australia and what is shared with the rest of the world. The many different ways in which this dialogue is regarded—the very diversity of Australian society—are themselves reflected in the Barton Lectures.

Individually and collectively 'the Bartons' have made a significant contribution to Australia's national conversation, and they will remain an important record of Australian ideas as we close one century and enter another. This book brings the Barton Lectures together, with two special contributions. Geoffrey Bolton explores the life and legacy of Edmund Barton and Elaine Thompson traverses the major political and social shifts in the twentieth century that provide the context for the lectures.

The NSW Centenary of Federation Committee is to be applauded for recognising the importance of such discussions and for supporting and organising these lectures. The ABC—itself a product of Federation—and the NSW Centenary Committee have together taken this contribution forward and have now made the Barton Lectures lastingly available to the public. Historians in the future, as well the interested public today, will without question be immensely grateful for the original idea of the Bartons and for the work that has enabled them to be completed.

HELEN IRVING
November 2001

Contents

FOREWORD HELEN IRVING   v

1   Something fishy in the mainstream?
    DONALD HORNE   1
2   Class in the year 2001 BELINDA PROBERT   20
3   The cities or the bush: Is that the real problem?
    RICK FARLEY   46
4   Challenges to egalitarianism: Diversity or
    sameness? ELAINE THOMPSON   69
5   The new differences between women
    LOIS BRYSON   88
6   More or less diverse JOHN HIRST   110
7   Recognising diversity MARY KALANTZIS   130
8   Recognition of the past... Reconciliation in
    the future... Restitution now LYDIA MILLER   149
9   Similar diversity: The Australian states and the
    Australian nation GREG CRAVEN   170
10 Australia's constitutional identity: A conundrum
    for the 21st century HELEN IRVING   194

AFTERWORDS
Edmund Barton revisited GEOFFREY BOLTON   221
The Australian Commonwealth: One hundred years
of continuity and change ELAINE THOMPSON   237

THE CONTRIBUTORS   253

1

Donald Horne

Something fishy in the mainstream?

Political phrases come and go. The phrase 'mainstream Australia' is at present part of our political vocabulary, but if you had come up to Edmund Barton when he was Australia's first prime minister a hundred years ago and asked him for his views on 'mainstream Australia' he would probably have assumed that you wanted to chat about the Murray–Darling river basin. It would be decades before 'mainstream' became a popular term for dominant concepts of an imagined national identity (and 'national identity' is another phrase that Barton would also never have heard, because it hadn't been invented).

He would have taken it as a matter of course that there were feelings of difference within the newly created Commonwealth. After all, it was because of the perceived differences between regions that the Commonwealth was a federation and had a constitution that provided for the creation of new states, and it was a time when anti-city feeling could be expressed with greater acrimony than any Hansonite could muster. If you had mentioned women, Barton would have known that they had been created different. He knew about class warfare, although he also knew about aspirations to civilise it. And being an Australian politician, he would have been very much alive to the sectarian hatreds between Protestants and Catholics. As to the Aborigines, he might not have bothered to mention them; in the debates on federation the indigenous people were scarcely discussed.

Barton would have hoped that the sense of being Australian overcame these differences—not 'Australian' in the terms of the bush nationalism that was developing in the 1890s, but in terms of the civic nationalism associated with some of the speech-making and poetry-making of the nineteenth-century federation movement that expired not long after Federation was born. But he also would have known that two great faiths were shared by most Australians: their membership of a 'White Australia' and their membership of the British Empire and 'the British race'. You can't begin to understand recent discontents unless you see them as residues—the first of them noxious—from these past faiths.

By the standard of the times Barton was restrained when he said, 'I do not think that the doctrine of the equality of man was really ever intended to include racial equality between the Englishman and the Chinaman'. What was to become the White Australia immigration policy was then seen by those who preferred to speak in rational terms as liberal and democratic in aspiration, based on the latest scientific evidence and wisely concerned with the political, social, economic, moral and cultural well-being of Australians. But there weren't many who spoke like that. The language in which the race-based immigration policy was expressed more usually drew, often lavishly and luridly, on the lexicon of vilification. What is now graffiti language was then part of public discourse. William Lane, the utopian labour writer, did not show Barton's restraint when he said: 'I would rather see my daughter dead in her coffin than kissing a black man on the mouth'. Nor did the cultivated literary critic A.G. Stephens when he wrote, 'Next in importance to the preservation of the national life is the purification of the national blood'. Nor did *The Bulletin* writer who lampooned the Chinese as 'not morally or physically or intellectually fit to sit down in the same continent as Europeans'. The policy was to become ingrained as a principal definition of Australia. When W.M. Hughes came back from the Treaty of Paris in 1919 as a triumphant prime minister, he said that Australians had died 'to maintain those ideals which we have nailed to the very topmost of our flagpole—White Australia, and those other aspirations of this young democracy'.

Now for Britishness. I think the following anecdote says it. In 1878 the schoolteacher Peter Dodds McCormick wrote 'Advance Australia Fair'. It caught on so firmly that it was sung by a choir of 10,000 at the inauguration of the Commonwealth in 1901 and was played by mass bands at the naming-of-Canberra ceremony in 1907. I'd like to remind you of the words of its now unsung last stanza:

When gallant Cook from Albion sailed,
To trace wide oceans o'er,
True British courage bore him on
Till he landed on our shore.
And there he raised old England's flag,

The standard of the brave.
With all her faults we love her still.
Britannia rule the waves!

When 10,000 people sang that stanza in 1901 no one laughed. No one laughed when massed bands played it in 1907 at the naming-of-Canberra ceremony. No one laughed when my school friends and I used to sing it on Empire Day at Muswellbrook District Rural School in the early 1930s along with those other patriotic Australian airs 'Rule, Britannia', 'Land of Hope and Glory' and 'Three Cheers for the Red, White and Blue'. With ritualised rhetoric, sacred phrases, historical tales, imperial slogans and iconic images, these patriotic airs also ingrained a principal definition of an Australia linked to Britain by 'the crimson thread of kinship', and still so strong that in December 1941, fifty years after Henry Parkes coined that phrase, John Curtin's first call was not to 'look to America' but to preserve in Australia 'the British-speaking race'. Some day someone should write a book about all this. Having replaced the muddled, romantically ahistorical and ethnologically and linguistically ill-based idea of an 'Anglo-Celtic' heritage with the more useful idea of a 'British and Irish heritage' the book could present the diverse and sometimes contradictory folk heritages that came out with the English, Irish, Scottish and Welsh people who were for so long the dominant immigrants and who, in ways we don't know much about, negotiated common styles and common differences that came to be seen as Australian. Racism would be there in the book, not only as in 'the white race' but also as in 'the British race' and 'the Anglo-Saxon race', chosen by God for their civilising missions. And xenophobia would be there, as

Australia faithfully followed, unaltered, the various British ways of despising 'Continentals'. There was the imperialism of the exciting bigness of Empire, with school-textbook world geography partly revolving around British naval coaling stations and items of empire trade; and there was the imperialism of alliance, sharing honour and self-interest with a great power (with such a powerful belief in loyalty that it would easily transfer to the United States when the time came); and there was the glamour of the many cultures of the Empire, with their many exotic ways. There were also the links with Britain that, for those who wanted this, provided intimations of a broader European civilisation as well as the literature, science and speculative thought of Britain itself (along with some very England-centred history). This was the greatest benefit of the British connection, even if it could produce among some Australians a cultural cringe or a cultural strut. But there was also a kind of High Britishry, created over 130 years in the eighteenth and early nineteenth centuries, described by Linda Colley in her book *Britons*[1] as a story of Protestant, imperial, military and constitutional ascendancy. These days a small, residual Australian Britishry still holds fast to the idea that the monarchy and certain other English institutions are simply part of the ordinary business of being Australian.

Now I'll put in an interlude. It is December 1960, and I have just taken over the editorship of *The Bulletin*, which, in a contradictory metaphor, had turned into a living museum of decaying attitudes—attitudes soon to be swept out of public sight throughout Australia, and to be swept out of *The Bulletin* in a couple of months. The slogan on its leader page was still 'Australia for the White Man'. (In a more rabid period it had been, 'Australia for the Australians. The cheap Chinaman, the cheap Nigger, and the cheap European pauper to be absolutely excluded'.) The first thing we did was to pluck that out of the page and throw it into the waste bin. We no longer ran pieces on topics such as how the newspapers were 'making pets of Colombo Plan Asian students' and in general we put an end to the self-proclaimed campaign of (to quote) 'keeping Australia racially in one piece'. We cut out the Abo jokes and the girlie jokes (DENTIST TO YOUNG WOMAN WITH UPLIFT: *'When I said what lovely falsies I was only referring to your teeth'*) and the reffo jokes. We no longer commissioned weekly articles such as the one that said that groups of immigrants from 'places like Cyprus, Poland and the depressed toe of Italy', each living in 'its national enclave, sticking to its racist and religious habits', were challenging 'the fibre of Australians' and 'weakening our British ties'. Or how 'occasionally some Continental lashes out at a crowd with an axe or wipes out a family', committing 'horrifying crimes unknown to Australians'. And *The Bulletin* was also a depository of the stereotype of Australians as a people of the bush (with the Digger as a lad from the bush in military uniform and the Bondi lifesaver as a lad from the bush in a cossie), of true Aussies defined by certain kinds of landscape paintings and black and white sketches, certain kinds of rural ballads and short stories, certain kinds of nature verse, certain kinds of fauna and certain modes of expression.

This was the very time when Australia was on the edge of a great, politically bipartisan sweep of change, running through the three post-Menzies Liberal governments, the Whitlam government and the Fraser government—with the beginnings of reform of the White Australia immigration policy, followed only a few years later by its abolition, by the abandonment of a narrowly defined assimilationist policy towards immigrants and its replacement by acceptance of a more hybrid Australia (preceded, incidentally, by a quick end to the old Protestant–Catholic sectarianism) and by the recognition of the indigenous peoples as part of the Australian polity, with a new indigenous agenda. It was also the time of a graduated turning away from Britain as the British left the map west of Suez and entered Europe, as Australia gained new trading partners, as the cultural cringe straightened out, as our horizons of international sightseeing broadened and as some scholars, journalists, intellectuals, government officials and a few politicians began to theorise about Australian relations with Asian countries.

Allowing for the necessary inadequacies of politics, this period of change was an enlightened and liberal period in Australian life, much of it initiated by circumstance or from activists outside politics, but one in which politicians played a mature and honourable role. They provided public leadership (an earlier example was Arthur Calwell's promulgation in 1949 of the newly coined phrase, 'New Australian' as a possible alternative to slurs such as 'dago', 'wog', 'reffo', etc). And, although there was no declared pact, there was an effective bipartisanship in which neither side in politics seized party political advantage by hinting at racist, ethnic or xenophobic prejudice. It was also one in which, overall, our citizens showed more tolerance and more common sense than they had been given credit for. This would also be worth a book—one that might end by speculating on why some of our fellow citizens then began to look backwards.

One should add that all these great social changes were accompanied by what may be the most significant social revolution of all—the continuing redefinitions of the roles of women: in the workplace, at home, in intellectual and artistic life, in recreation and in their sexual lives. What's more, there was a rapid overturning of censorship and a rapid decolonising of the Australian artistic, intellectual and scholarly imaginations. These were overwhelming the old stereotypes still dominant in *The Bulletin* before I took it over, and to such effect that in the 'Tin Symphony' section of the opening ceremony at the 2000 Olympic Games these legends and stereotypes were presented as matters of whimsy. When we got to the Centennial Park evening ceremony on 1 January 2001, a ten-year-old boy of Sri Lankan origin was one of those who spoke up for Australia.

With such changes things seemed to be going along all right, but another great national faith had also been challenged, one with an importance that is not even yet understood. This was the faith, conceptualised in the 1880s, in national economic development. It was seen as a common enterprise, almost a secular crusade, in which all Australians might contribute, and from which all Australians might expect a return. It was a faith that seemed at times threatened, especially in two great depressions but, if it makes sense to speak of people being held together, it was a force that helped hold Australians together in something that almost all of them could seem to share and that provided a basis for many of their hopes and fears. And it had a long run in national rhetoric. 'From being a wild, uncultured waste, so poor and barren that the first explorers shrank back aghast,' Cardinal Moran had written in 1883, 'Australia has become a civilised land, clothed with loveliness as a garden'. And in his 1909 *Short History of Australia* A.W. Jose had written that we must take seriously in hand 'the development of the country's natural resources'. To do this 'methodically, scientifically' was 'Australia's task for the future. Young Australians cannot serve their country better than by preparing themselves with zealous study to take their share in the task directly they become men.' New images of national development were to arise alongside the established images of minefield and farm. In the drained swamps beside Newcastle harbour went up the blast furnaces and mills and chimney stacks of the BHP; between the wars motor vehicle assembly lines, glassworks, textile mills emerged; after World War II the Holden, 'Australia's Own Car' was launched in 1948 as a symbol of national achievement. A visit to the ferro-concrete of the Snowy River Scheme became a national pilgrimage. There was the modernity and progress of manufacturing our own consumer goods; our own Rothman's King Size Filter cigarettes; our own Sunbeam Electric frypans; Qantas Empire Airways dropped the 'Empire' from its name then internationalised itself as Australia's international airline. This national faith was last seen in the Whitlam government's and then the Fraser government's speeches on the resources boom.

This firmest of Australian wisdoms—the belief in development at any cost—seemed to be challenged by the growth of an environmentalist movement, but environmentalism was discussable. What finished it (giving it no new meaning) were the puzzles of becoming something called 'The Economy', an abstract idea that took over in the mid 1980s and began to communicate with us, remotely, in terms of economic indicators released in graphics on television. Unlike national development, this Economy was not something of which we could feel a part. Of course, as we moved into the post-industrial society the old economies were falling to bits and remaking themselves in new forms all over the prosperous world, but faith in national development was so ingrained in Australian national definition that the abandonment of this belief might have weakened our holding together. There was a sense of loss made more real because no one came up with a revised version, and made most real because no leading politician was able to appear sympathetic to the unprecedented jolts and uncertainties in the workforce. With things shaken up without credible explanation and an accompanying collapse in political rhetoric there was, among some Australians, a turning back to bits and pieces of the old faith. It was this turning back that, if you judge it by its immediate effects, made Pauline Hanson's 1996 maiden speech possibly the most effective maiden speech ever made in the Australian parliament. Partly as a result of the prime minister's failure to do anything about it, it had instant results.

It was at this time that, instead of speaking, in a way we were getting used to, of a diverse Australia made up of many strands, Australians began to hear the words 'mainstream' and 'minority interests' as if Australians were divided into two main classes. There was the main mob, a uniform class of good, worthy real Australians (whose grandparents might have laughed at the old *Bulletin*'s Abo and reffo jokes), and there were the breakaways, a threatening rabble of *un*-Australians. There was a dirty name for these dissidents: it was 'minority interests'. They were, however, a special kind of 'minority interest'. They weren't natural minority interests like cotton farmers or war veterans or people living under airline flight paths, they were members of 'the Aboriginal industry' or 'the multicultural industry', or 'the welfare industry', or 'femocrats' or 'econuts'. Of course there is nothing unusual in calling your opponents funny names. But the mainstream idea was producing concepts of an Australian normality that made it un-Australian for certain kinds of people to put up a case for themselves. That was a privilege applying only to some groups, and if it applied to them they weren't really 'minority groups' (although of course they were).

It brought head-on one of the conundrums of democracy. Representative democracy isn't in any classic sense democracy. It is just the best we can do: it leads to a peaceful handing over of power and it means that holding elections can provide some kind of a check on government (although it may not). But we should recognise that when we cast our votes on election day we aren't participants in government. We are simply voters choosing between two or more highly oligarchic party structures (although there can be conflicts among the oligarchs). We can urge efficient balloting (something in which all mature representative governments could teach the United States a lesson). We can urge that a government shouldn't gain office when clearly a majority of voters don't want it: something in which a number of countries can teach Australia a lesson. But ancient Athens we aren't. (Nor in many ways, of course, was ancient Athens.) Where democracy comes into it—liberal democracy, anyway—goes beyond voting. This exists when we have a chance of putting our views forward in any legal way we choose, and lobbying for our special interests as hard as we can. To recognise the mosaic of minority interests that makes up any modern society is an essential of modern liberal democracy. The alternative view (from the muddy bottom of the mainstream) that the majority is always right is illiberal and authoritarian. We all belong to the political state called the Commonwealth of Australia, of a liberal-democratic, pluralist kind (summoned into existence in the late 1890s by a vote from its future citizens). We do not belong to a 'nation' ethnically cleansed of all but arbitrarily defined 'typical Australians'.

There has always been in Australia a lurking fear that the whole place might fall apart unless we are all, as near as possible, the same. Given the fact that we are *not* all 'typical Australians' it seems prudent to look for other reasons for imagining why, so far, Australian society has not fallen apart. One useful idea, far different from the popular range of caricatures, is that one essential in holding together is to recognise that the harmony of a society depends partly on accepting the presence of minority interests in that society—cotton farmers, single mothers, RSL branches, Slovene clubs. It depends partly on seeing the differences and the conflicts between them and on recognising in these an essential element in a liberal democracy. Or as Professor John Anderson used to say: 'A variety of organisations is a condition of social life'. Or—even better—as Benedict de Spinoza, the seventeenth-century conceptualiser of tolerance, used to say three hundred years before John Anderson came from Glasgow University to the University of Sydney in the 1920s: 'Since it is impossible to coerce thought, the way to sustain social harmony is to discuss conflict and pursue truth. The more people speak their minds freely, the more they are likely to be loyal citizens.' It is not uniformity that produces an harmonious society, neither by physical suppression nor by coercion of opinion. It is by the acceptance of *difference*, an acquaintance with its perils and its virtues and, humans being what they are, its inevitability. Anything else is, at its most severe, oppressive and divisive; and, at its least, superficial and trifling.

For this kind of understanding, in Australia we have to consider in particular two words. One is used too often, the other not often enough. The first word is 'equality', the second is 'tolerance'.

The meaning of 'equality' in Australia has always had within it a tendency towards uniformity, assuming at its worst a lowest-common-denominator equality. 'Equality' is a hard word to get down precisely on paper. Its meaning can be expressed most clearly in rights of legal process or in elementary civic rights (universal voting, for example) and, despite the practical difficulties, in the principles of equal opportunity and, despite the definitional difficulties, in prohibitions of discrimination based on sex, religious creed, age, race or ethnicity. Some positive, aspirational 'rights' may move beyond the possible. (Rights to full employment, for example.) But there are those dangerous moments when equality becomes not a legal matter at all, but the respectable face of envy. Over the last few years we have had those who are envious of people on the dole, even envious of indigenous people as a kind of new privileged class. Perhaps there will soon be a movement demanding—in the name of a fair go—equal access for all Australians to night refuges and soup kitchens. In any society there must be hundreds of special cases, perhaps thousands. A sensible and humane egalitarian does not demand that there be no special cases, but that when it comes to special cases there should be a concern of fairness within them.

As to tolerance: given what was once the almost universal use of colour of skin as a definition of Australia, tolerance didn't build up much of a past history, except in the legal religious tolerance that accompanied a fierce sectarianism—an important and fruitful exception. Otherwise tolerance was to mean little more than shrugging off certain kinds of amusing human frailties. (And, at a time of high wowserism, government censorship and police enforcement of approved theories of sexual conduct, the list of sustainable frailties was limited.) There is another problem now that 'tolerance' has come into use in the last couple of decades: some people have attacked it as patronising, even as an expression of white Anglo-Saxon superiority. This misses the point. Tolerance doesn't mean that we love or respect each other. It means that, in accepting a plurality of values and ways of being human, we accept the right to difference even of people we loathe. (And it goes far beyond attitudes towards the indigenous peoples or 'ethnics'.) It's a way of getting on with each other, even when we *don't* respect each other. There is another quotation from Spinoza: 'To tolerate a group who follow a system of belief or a way of life is not a question of liking, or approving, or agreeing with them. It is a question of accepting their right to be there. Being tolerant means you accept people's right to (lawfully) do or say what they like. It also means you have the right to criticise them as stringently as you wish.' He might have added that it also means you accept their right to criticise you.

Of course, people have all kinds of feelings of belonging. One of the greatest of these—the faith in a shared national economic development—has now disappeared as a comprehensible experience. Some Australians are still somewhat obsessed by, or at least feel they should go along with, definitions of Australia as a patriotic landscape of blue hills, gum trees and kangaroos. Others have made themselves at home by turning it into a landscape of threatened wilderness areas uneasily inhabited by endangered species. People can accept flags and national anthems, most take pride in whatever Australian history stories have come their way, or in recent Australian achievements (even if mainly sporting achievements). Living in a modern consumer society, many of them share the make-believe of advertising and the demands of the shopping experience, and as a mass entertainment society they take their pick from the same range of entertainment in the TV serials, news programs and sporting programs. Some feel they belong because they have maintained some of the habits of their homelands in a new country. And there are all kinds of individual feelings about being Australian that can mean most to Australians because they are *local*—about the places where they live and the people they live with. I like to think that there are certain characteristics—essentially superficial, and that's an important part of it—that are often found in the ways Australians deal with each other in public and are one of the things many people have in common. The passage of the Olympic flame was a great example—all these different kinds of people from so many different parts of the country passing on the same flame.

And Australia has a civil society, the social space beyond that which is occupied by the state, the place where most people, whether as individuals or groups, get on with much of what interests them and most of the things over which they have some control, and also something a bit different from that: what Martin Krygier in his 1997 Boyer Lectures[2] called 'civil trust', of 'trust among people who don't and can't know each other intimately but still make judgements, however abstract, about the extent to which they can rely on each other'. If you compare the ideas of 'civil society' and 'civil trust' with the repertoire of nationalist caricatures—of Australians as koalas or gum trees, or as the Man from the Snowy River or as Don Bradman or as Simpson and his Donkey—these two civic ideas can seem a bit humdrum, not sufficiently 'distinctive' from all those other liberal-democratic countries: after all, they also have civil societies and civil trust. But sometimes what is distinctive (however important—and it is vitally important, because it's about giving a local habitation and a name) may matter less than what is more general.

There is another side to it. Some of what is most distinctive in Australia can seem too ordinary to talk about, in particular the long history in Australia of being suburban and, as at least Australian movies demonstrate, the diversity of suburban experience. This may provide many more clues to Australian comparative social harmony than much of the rhetoric about mateship. The nineteenth-century enthusiasm for mutuality—in friendly societies, housing societies, temperance societies, trade societies—is almost forgotten, yet it meant more to ordinary living in the cities and suburbs and towns than (except among some men in certain kinds of workplaces) mateship.

But any society contains xenophobes, racists, zealots, bigots, ratbags and other merchants of repressive hatred, often people more inflamed by social envy and resentment than most of us.

This brings up a particular aspect of maintaining social harmony that we don't hear much about. In a liberal-democratic society, political leaders need to do constant boundary riding to make sure that the main political system is not infected by such pestilence. Politicians live by division: they live, partly, on dividing the country. But they have to know where to stop. Politicians' setting of examples in reducing prejudice over the last few decades may now be derided as 'political correctness' by some, but if the harmony of a society depends partly in recognising the existence of minority interests, we should celebrate as a great collective performance the period of effective political bipartisanship from the mid 1960s to the late 1980s, when our politicians refused to use appeals to certain prejudices as a way of gaining political advantage. And we must regret its ending.

At present we are confronted by two failures in political rhetoric. One is its failure in the last twenty years to find a substitute for the faith in national development. It offered people a nationally unifying notion, made up (like the British Empire in its grand days) both of emotion (sometimes even bad poetry) and self-interest. Even at times of economic depression, people could look forward to a return to normal. Now that faith has gone. There is no new 'normal', and no political leader is providing one. With this came, in the Howard years, an almost complete flattening-out in the general ability to articulate theories about what's going on in the world and in Australia, and to try to interest Australians in it.

The second failure is that most of our political leaders and a number of other public figures are incapable of using an Australian civic language when speaking to their fellow citizens—a failure that, depressingly, was demonstrated all too frequently in 2001 when top persons came together in the name of the centenary of the Commonwealth. It was a year in which there could have been a united effort in strengthening ways of talking about Australia as a *polity*, as a common civic enterprise. But retro-revivals of tired myths about 'national character' were preferred.

There continues to be a failure to use on appropriate occasions, as a matter of course, a *civic* definition of Australia instead of the fancifulness of 'national character' and 'national identity'. There is still a feeling that there are *ethnic* tests for being truly or typically Australian, whereas the only overall claim can be that we are all Australian citizens together and we make of it what we can. We still have no common language for speaking of the civic values that most Australians in fact share, even if they often don't have the words for them. I am not mad enough to believe, as a few critics have suggested, that this is all that 'holds us together', merely that one of the jobs of political leaders is to enunciate common civic values. Yes, it's true that 'We are One but we are [also] Many'. But while the 'many' is self-evident, why not speculate about what makes us one? Not bush landscapes. Not wide-brimmed hats. Not calling out, 'Oi, Oi, Oi'. What answer can there be except a statement about our basic faiths as a political community? The Commonwealth of Australia is not an ethnic entity. What we are expected to hold in common—and what, very largely, we do hold in common—is a civic faith. Where is the danger in articulating it, in talking about what that civic faith might be?

This faith is not hard to put into words, although the imagination with which the words can be used would vary according to taste. An opening assumption might be that the government itself comes under the law, and that the law should be administered predictably and fairly and with respect for the equality under the law of all Australians. There should be, of course, a declaration that Australia is a liberal parliamentary democracy based on a universal franchise carried out in fair elections and with freedom of opinion. There could also be a commitment to upholding Australia as a tolerant society and as a fair society devoted to the well-being of its people. And since this is Australia, there could also be a recognition of the unique status of the Aboriginal and Torres Strait Islander peoples. Something like this might be seen as the basis of being an Australian.

And the alternative? What should we call someone who believes that the government is above the law, that opinion should be standardised, that majorities are born to rule, that minorities endanger social cohesion, that the well-being of the Australian people is not a concern of government, and that there was not a prior Aboriginal occupation of Australia? One might almost be tempted—although of course one would resist the temptation—to call such a person 'un-Australian'.

ENDNOTES

1. Linda Colley, *Britons: Forging the Nation 1707–1837*, Yale University Press, Boston, 1992.
2. Martin Krygier, *Between Fear and Hope: Hybrid Thoughts on Public Values*, ABC Books, Sydney, 1997.

BELINDA PROBERT

Class in the year 2001

It is only right and proper that an English migrant should be asked to talk about class in the year 2001. An English upbringing ensures an acute awareness of class—not just as a system of material inequalities but also as a particular kind of social differentiation that permeates people's daily lives. It is not only about difference, of course, but also pride, snobbery, the desire to be in a higher class and, increasingly, the fear of falling into a lower one. In British TV comedies, Mrs Bucket who wishes to be known as Mrs Bouquet, Audrey in *To the Manor Born*, the East Enders and inhabitants of Coronation Street all play on an assumed and agreed-upon hierarchy of classes. Hyacinth Bucket is funny precisely because of her refusal to acknowledge the impossibility of social mobility.

When I arrived in Australia in 1976 to teach at Murdoch University in Western Australia, the first people to invite me to their home for dinner were the departmental secretary and her husband, a fitter and turner. They instructed me to bring a plate, and when I brought an empty plate under the misapprehension that they did not have enough crockery for a large dinner, they mocked me dryly. It could never have happened in my birthplace, the Home Counties.

As I began to read accounts of the distinctive qualities of Australian society that had been written in the 1950s and 1960s, they reinforced my own early experiences with their almost invariable insistence on the importance of egalitariansim as a form of expected behaviour. Some of them even asserted the non-existence of classes. The two images that appeared in almost every popular work concerned the way Australians could be counted on to respond to meetings with the plumber and opportunities to ride in a taxi, as in: 'The man who comes to your house to mend a broken pipe ... will ... go out of his way to help if you appeal to him as one man to another, but will take offence if you address him as master to servant'. Or, in another version: 'If the plumber calls to mend the sink it's imperative to offer him a cup of tea'. Taxi riding etiquette is an even more popular exemplar of Australian egalitariansim, as in references to 'the almost universal custom of sitting beside the driver in the front of a taxi if you are alone'. This image is used by John Pringle in 1958, Donald Horne in 1964, Craig McGregor in his 1966 *Profile of Australia* and by the then Liberal premier of New South Wales who declared in 1967 that 'we have no poor people in New South Wales. Nor any very rich people. Ours is a classless society. That's why we ride in the front seat of the taxi.'[1]

The sociologist Bob Connell, who has traced the taxi image through its innumerable incarnations, thinks it all began with the taxi driver who appears in the opening pages of D.H. Lawrence's novel *Kangaroo*, a novel written after a fleeting visit to Australia in 1922. The novel begins with a bewildered Englishman attempting to engage a taxi driver in Sydney, only to find that the driver is not interested in the job at threepence a bag, 'Shilling apiece, them bags,' says the driver, 'laconically'. Mr Somers' wife finds the taxi driver *'vile'*, but Mr Somers understands something about Australia. 'It's God's Own Country, as they always tell you . . . [In] a free country, it's the man who makes you pay who is free—free to charge you what he likes, and you're forced to pay it. That's what freedom amounts to. They're free to charge, and you are forced to pay.'[2]

Classes did, of course, exist. People lived in working-class or middle-class suburbs; they shared different patterns of income and opportunity determined by their position in the labour market. Class meant different patterns of consumption and different attitudes to many things. Class was a way of explaining how the world worked. Class was power—or the lack of it. But in the 1950s and 1960s in Australia (and even in Britain) enough was happening to make a great many people think that classes didn't matter any more.

In Australia, the widely shared experience of being able to buy your own home, find secure employment whenever you wished and bring up a family on one wage created a general sense of well-being, and rendered class-based explanations of individual lives increasingly irrelevant. By the early 1960s four out of every five private houses were owner-occupied, or at least purchaser-occupied.[3] Over half of all employees belonged to a union, and most of these voted Labor—for pragmatic reasons rather than ideological ones. Being working-class was not a condition that needed to be abolished or even radically altered. Even in Britain, sociologists were wondering whether the growing affluence of groups like vehicle builders was not eroding the differences in attitudes and behaviour that had been such visible manifestations of class. Was the man in the Vauxhall car plant becoming increasingly bourgeois? they asked. In Australia, opinion surveys consistently found that over half of all Australians considered themselves to be middle-class, far more than any objective measure would allow.[4]

It was not simply the rising levels of widely shared affluence that made class so unimportant. It was the result of the particular way in which the bitter class warfare of the late nineteenth century had been resolved at the time of Federation. Australia, the nation, was established in a climate of widely shared values about the national purpose, with specific legislation and public institutions that embodied these values. When Barton, Deakin and Labor leaders like Spence spoke about 'fairness' they were talking about the same sort of thing. They meant that the living standards of Australian families should be protected through wage regulation, and in this way all Australians would develop into citizens. As Deakin put it in 1906:

The best thing that Australians could do was to make the country so productive, so good a place to live, and bring about such just and fair conditions, with such fair opportunities for earning an honest living, such protection against monopolies, with such fair chances for all men who were prepared to go on the land and work for industries, that other people would also want to become Australians.[5]

Other Barton lecturers have pointed out that this fairness did not extend to Aborigines or other races. Nor did it extend to women. Its significance related only to class. But this was a remarkable and enduring consensus nonetheless. Ten years earlier the situation could only have been described as one of class warfare. Not only were one-third of all skilled workers unemployed, but the employers and the colonial governments seemed bent on destroying the power of the unions, using police and soldiers where necessary.

But out of these bitter struggles came lasting institutions and practices, not just fine words, that delivered a distinctive kind of fairness to many Australian families. Central to these were the Australian Labor Party—Australia's oldest political party—and the system of industrial arbitration. It took a little longer for the anti-labour classes to organise themselves, but Federation marked the point at which the rather fragmented colonial politics became organised into a relatively rigid two-party system based on class loyalties.[6] Class conflict could not be abolished, as it is inevitable in any capitalist economy. But from 1904 it was to be managed through a judicial process, and a special court would decide between the claims and counterclaims of employers and employees.

When Justice Higgins announced that Australian workers were to be paid a fair and reasonable wage based on a family's normal needs, rather than whatever they could extract out of a power struggle with their employer, this most Australian of class compromises was made legitimate. Employers who could not pay a decent wage were not welcome in Australia. There are bosses and there are workers, but in the court they are just parties to a dispute. As John Rickard so eloquently puts it:

Arbitration is the most explicit statement possible of the Australian belief that Jack is as good as his master. This does not of course alter their roles; indeed it is based on the assumption that

Jack will remain Jack. Arbitration has not only institutionalised conflict in Australian society, it has also institutionalised some of Australia's most cherished beliefs (and prejudices) about itself and life in general.[7]

Jack was not really as good as his master. Egalitarianism was primarily a matter of manners. There was indeed widespread respect for hard manual labour in a country where sheep and gold were so important. The shearer, for example, came in for adulation and mythologising. But none of this had much impact on the material gulf that continued to exist between the incomes, homes and education of the major classes.

In Australia, class-consciousness remained distinctively labourist. There was little support for the establishment of a more radical social democracy or a full-blown welfare state. What we did get after the Great Depression and World War II was a genuine policy commitment to full employment for men, and financial support for dependent wives and children. A job and a family were to be the key to working-class security.[8]

I now realise that when I arrived in Australia in 1976 these distinctively Australian class relationships were beginning to unravel. Every political science textbook still talked about the party structure as 'Labor and non-Labor', and in 1977 an eminent professor of political science wrote confidently that class remained the key to voting patterns.[9] But in 1978 another young professor, David Kemp, who was shortly to begin a political career that later found him as a Liberal minister in the Howard government, published research to show that class and party were fracturing.[10] This was probably premature, as it was not until the 1990s that significant elements of the working class felt politically abandoned. Certainly in the 1960s the sentiment of egalitarianism was still dominant and the normative framework that underpinned widespread acceptance of the notion of a basic wage was alive and well. In one of its finer, if belated, moments, the arbitration system delivered legislative equal pay for women.

Equally striking to an English migrant was the absence, then, of an immigrant underclass. It still gives me a small sense of Australianness when I return to Tullamarine airport and see a white man cleaning the floor. Arriving at Heathrow in London the connections between immigration, race and low pay are immediately revealed as a Pakistani immigrant hovers in the women's toilets. The massive immigration program of the postwar years did indeed lead to the creation of migrant jobs in Australia—often dirty jobs, but generally unionised jobs, with legally enforceable minimum wage rates. Centralised wage fixing meant that there were no regional wage variations or opportunities for employers to create 'pockets' of cheap labour. It also meant that wage rises won in one sector or industry rapidly spread to others, migrant-dominated or not.[11] In other words, the male working class remained, by and large, 'the working class', rather than developing into segments or fragments or other kinds of hierarchically ordered layers. Even the expansion of white-collar occupations and rising levels of education did little to alter the class structure, with white-collar workers joining unions, just like their blue-collar brothers.

The sense of predictability and acceptance that accompanied the class structure is captured in the way this human resource manager from the Shepparton region remembers schools preparing people for work in the 1960s:

I went to school at the local high school, and everyone knew how it worked. There were kids who left school at the end of the third form and they went into trades or labouring-type jobs. Others left at the end of fourth form and went into a bank, or worked for the SEC or local government. The ones that finished fifth form went teaching or nursing. The nerds who completed sixth form, or matric as it was then, went to uni.[12]

The majority would not complete high school, and it didn't seem to matter. However, when I finally crossed the Nullabor and arrived in Melbourne in 1980 I was surprised to find one vital element of the British class system alive and well—namely, a relatively well patronised private school system.

Classes today

Looking back from 2001, it is hard to know which is the more remarkable: the stability of the class compromise achieved at Federation or the speed with which it has unravelled over the last twenty years. The economic pressures and the ideas used to justify the dismantling of egalitarian structures and sentiment are not unique to Australia, but Australia turned out to be far more vulnerable to these pressures and ideas than, for example, the European social democracies. Nor should Australians be encouraged to confine their comparative gaze to our English-speaking relatives on either side of the Atlantic. They are unworthy competitors, and it would be a race to the bottom. In a recent comparison of the degree of income inequality across twenty-one wealthy countries, the United States came out top (or worst), Britain was not far behind and Australia was sixth.[13] I think most Australians are shocked by facts such as these.

Australians may yet prove more determined to protect the key values of fairness and decency expressed by all parties one hundred years ago than our Anglophone relatives. I hope so. I didn't take out Australian citizenship in order to protect my place in the sunshine. I took it out because I like those things that are now under threat.

The pressures that have now fractured the old class settlement are well known. They include the increasingly inefficient nature of some Australian production; the increasingly competitive international markets in which many firms now have to do business; the decline of many traditional industries and the rise of new ones requiring different kinds of workers; rising unemployment and the push for equal employment opportunities for women. Two major bipartisan policy decisions—to abolish tariff protection and to deregulate the financial system—signalled the radical nature of the changes to come. And in their wake was a host of policy moves that had one common effect—namely, increasing the exposure of the Australian working class to market forces and winding back mechanisms and policies designed to regulate these forces in the name of fairness or decency.

Within a very short period we were being asked to choose between economic growth and sustained prosperity on the right hand and redistributive policies based on egalitarian values on the left. It was a case of drown together in a sea of unsustainable egalitarian mediocrity or free the entrepreneurial spirit from social responsibilities so that we might all rise on a tide of creative destruction. The welfare state, which had embodied a particular kind of class compromise, became a 'burden' on the economy. A new moral economy found expression in such phrases as 'the winner takes all' while 'battlers' became 'losers', and the unemployed were to 'price themselves' into a job. The changes were presented as inevitable—the TINA syndrome: There Is No Alternative. The fact that other small open economies like Denmark and Holland managed both growth and equity was not allowed to get in the way of the new story. America was to be the constant point of comparison.

Many elements of Australia's historical class compromise went by the wayside, including regulated home loans. But in terms of the impact on Australia's class structure and class relations, the biggest revolution has been the abandonment of full employment as an achievable goal and the frontal attack on unions, arbitration and centralised wage fixing. These have been central factors in the fragmentation of the Australian community, and the detachment[14] or marginalisation of significant segments of the population from the mainstream regulatory and social protection mechanisms. The 'wage-earners' welfare state', as it has been called, has been increasingly unable to protect large sections of the community from growing insecurity and inequality.

Much of the debate about the new class structure, in Australia as well as in Britain and the United States, focuses on what has happened at the bottom end. During the 1990s, for example, we discovered that the unemployed had become detached from the rest of the working class and become a new and disturbingly large group to be called the 'long-term unemployed'. Closer examination of public expenditure on welfare payments revealed that the numbers of Australians receiving a range of different benefits had increased sharply. Taken together these elements began to fuse into something that was increasingly called an 'underclass'.

However, if we want to understand how classes work in general, and if we want to understand Australia's new class relations, we need to start at the top, with the interests of capital and the managers of capital in this rapidly changing economy. After all, some classes are more equal than others.

THE OVERCLASS

The employing class has been transformed. Some large employers now like to distance themselves from the greed, corruption and short-term horizons of the more famous entrepreneurs—the Bonds and Skases—who unleashed themselves onto the rest of us in the 1980s. But there was a more generalised shift in the priorities of employers that was used to justify the abandonment of the historical project of national development, the retreat from any commitment to employment security as the key to citizenship and the rejection of state interference in wage setting.

It was not only the language that changed. Accepting the arguments of the employers, the Industrial Relations Commission rejected the trade union movement's 1996 Living Wage Claim and with it the legacy of Justice Higgins, namely 'the idea that a socially acceptable living standard should be a feature of the Australian wage setting system'.[15]

Two years later small increases in the living wage were in fact granted, but the Commission acknowledged at the time that many low-paid workers were now struggling to make ends meet. Employees were pricing themselves into poverty. The rhetoric of egalitarianism went, along with mechanisms that had ensured some measure of it. Women workers, who had been given a brief taste of what could be achieved through the arbitration system once it took responsibility for equal pay, found themselves moving backwards again.

With the Industrial Relations Commission progressively sidelined from the process of settling disputes between capital and labour during the 1990s, we should probably not be surprised to see the re-emergence of the kind of naked class war that characterised the 1890s. Many people might not have noticed what happened when Rio Tinto took on the coalminers of the Hunter Valley and insisted on its right to continue the dispute rather than submit to a process of arbitration,[16] but everyone noticed when Patrick Stevedores set out to deunionise its workforce. Although the depth of community resistance to what was happening protected the union in this case, it was quite obvious that Jack was no longer to be treated as though he were as good as his master. And the trend to union-free workplaces has continued.[17] The net effect has been that increasing numbers of employees meet their employer on significantly weakened ground.

The employing class has also been improving its personal income relative to everyone else. While the wages and salaries of employees were held down in the interests of sustaining profits and economic growth, we saw the rewards for chief executives move onto an exponential growth path. John Prescott was taking home $2.3 million when he was CEO of BHP. When the AMP was privatised, George Trumbull got not only his $2.4 million salary but also a $7 million windfall from the float.[18] Shares and share options are increasingly likely to play a part in these remuneration packages.

There is also another emerging group in Australia who are likely to identify with the employers. Let's call the two parts together the 'overclass', a term invented by Robert Reich. This emergent part of the overclass is made up of those individuals who earn very large salaries or fees and invest in shares as a major source of longer-term security. They, like the other members of the overclass, have no use for the major institutions of the welfare state—public hospitals, public schools or pensions. They benefit from the short-term profit-seeking of highly mobile investment funds. The rise of performance-related pay and bonuses, rather than status-based salaries, helps to detach this group from more egalitarian workplace cultures. They are likely to believe that the public sector is a drain on the private sector's ability to generate wealth, however untrue this might be.

THE MIDDLE CLASS

Beneath the overclass we still have a middle class, defined increasingly by their tertiary educational credentials or cultural capital. This class is growing, as the new economy requires a lot of highly skilled managers, professionals and technicians (the fastest-growing occupational categories in the 1990s).[19] This is the group that Robert Reich calls 'symbolic analysts'—knowledge- or information-based workers who identify and solve problems.[20] The middle class includes more and less secure strata, of course. Some elements are a bit uncomfortable in the new era of 'fast capitalism'.[21] Some managers find they are still on the greasy pole at the age of forty when they expected to be comfortably established; some occupations—especially those in the public sector—have become much more stressful. Some, in this class, have had to trade off some security for increased pay. Some worry about the competition for middle-class jobs that their children face, so they are queuing up to send their children to private schools, in Victoria at least. And some of these private schools now take the children in at three months and keep them until they are ready for university. (Indeed, nearly every child at a private school stays on until Year 12, compared to only 65 per cent in government schools.)[22]

This class is also blessed by often having two middle incomes in the one household, for women with tertiary education have really been making advances in these kinds of educationally credentialled jobs. This is why they need the private school pre-school as well as after-school care. Their commitment to public education is probably now ideological rather than self-interested. This class also has private health insurance. It wishes it had more shares. Its members live in inner suburbs and have helped to push the value of housing in these areas through the roof. They are accumulating wealth that will later help to give their children access to these suburbs.

My own story shows how accidentally these middle-class changes can occur. On arriving in Melbourne I bought a wooden cottage in a good inner suburb. I bought it from a retired fitter and turner who had raised six children in its three bedrooms. I sold it for three times what I had paid for it, thirteen years later, and bought a dual-income larger version not far away. Property values in that street have shown a similar tendency to increase. The only serious impediment to the accumulation of wealth in this way, as every estate agent knows, is divorce.

At the same time the government's competition policy forced me to choose between my existing superannuation scheme that guaranteed me a reasonable retirement income if I behaved sensibly and a risky share option scheme that might make me a lot better off in my old age. Enough of the personal revelations here—my point is simply that middle-class people do not have to be ill-intentioned to find themselves increasingly aligned with the overclass and objectively detached from the interests of the underclass. They are increasingly ambivalent about redistributive taxation and the value of public utilities and public services because their standard of living is now more closely tied to the share market and property market.

The one element of the middle class that has never been ambivalent about redistributive taxation, but consistently opposed, is small business. But even this group has become more complex and differentiated. The self-employed are a steadily growing part of the Australian class structure, now making up 10 per cent of the working population.[23] But many of them are in fact constantly in danger of slipping into the underclass, grasping at self-employment because of the impact of outsourcing and downsizing. Much of the work relates to household tasks such as cleaning, gardening and home maintenance which the dual-income middle class can now afford to outsource.

The working class

As well as a middle class there is still a working class. The better-off segment of the working class have ongoing full-time employment (in theory at least), and they can join a union. Their employment conditions are still regulated by awards and enterprise bargaining in which unions have some influence. They get holiday pay and sick pay and can't be sacked on a whim. The more highly skilled element has managed to maintain its living standards, but the traditional working class is shrinking. In 2001 the working class are as likely to be bank, retail or call centre employees as factory workers and they are all working very long hours. For the majority, one wage is no longer enough to sustain the Australian dream.

The less well off segment of the working class is employed in non-unionised service industries, or those dominated by casual and part-time work such as hospitality and tourism, or they work for labour hire companies. It includes family breadwinners like Emma Barkley who has a full-time job cleaning rooms in an upmarket Melbourne hotel, for which she takes home $337 a week.[24] If they own a house, it may well be in a suburb with declining property values. They may work full-time but are in danger of sliding into the 'working poor'. Some of these people may best be understood as sharing the difficulties faced by the class below, but the trade union movement is now engaged in a critical struggle to draw them more tightly into the organised working class. Current campaigns around maternity leave for ongoing casual employees, and, in the metal trades, for the right to permanency after six months' casual employment may not sound earth-shattering. But they are vital indications of renewed commitment to finding a better class compromise.

The underclass

Most discussion about Australia's changing class structure has focused on the growth of a very large number of people whose material circumstances make them worse off than the traditional Australian working class, and who stand little chance of finding secure employment or buying a house. Not only this, but they will find their claims to welfare support increasingly challenged and contested. For the moment let's just call them the 'new underclass'—even though this term is disputed.

The thing that primarily defines this group is their tenuous relationship with employment. It includes the unemployed *and* the very insecurely employed; the people on various kinds of make-work schemes; the discouraged job seekers; the mothers who cannot afford childcare; the growing army of the working poor who rely on welfare support to survive; those on disability pensions who would work if appropriate jobs existed; those with part-time jobs who need a full-time income.

It is important to appreciate the sheer size of this new underclass. We can quibble about exactly who is in it and who isn't, but its outlines are clearly visible to anyone who wishes to see. Almost one-fifth of working-age people in Australia are now in sufficient strife to receive some kind of social security payment. The proportion in such need has doubled since I arrived in Australia.[25] That is now more than two and a half million people. If we look at those who do have employment, there are at least four overlapping categories who cannot be said to enjoy any of the traditional benefits of being a worker in Australia—those who are involuntarily working less than full-time; those employed in temporary jobs; those employed on a casual basis; and those whose hours vary at the whim of their employer. If we just look at short-term employment, this has grown to a quarter of all jobs. A cautious estimate would put this 'precariously' employed group at about two million.[26]

Households that manage to combine a working-class job with an underclass job can just about keep their heads above water. But just as the university-educated middle class tend to marry each other, so the unskilled and economically vulnerable tend to do the same. Hence the growing polarisation between what have been called 'work-rich households' and 'work-poor households'.[27] About 850,000 Australian children live in families where neither parent has a job.[28]

The four classes

There are greyish boundaries between all these classes, and they could be subdivided around finer distinctions. But even this rather crude description of four main classes allows us to think about the class system more generally. The most striking feature is that the material gaps between them and the gaps in political interest are getting wider by the minute. And these inequalities are further exaggerated by the increasingly geographic concentration of classes, driven largely by the housing market and the private/public school division.

Understandings of Class

If the objective underpinnings of the Australian class system have been transformed over the last twenty years, it should not surprise us that attitudes to class have also been turned upside down. In particular, we don't seem to know how to make sense of this new underclass.

But let's start with the traditional working class. The historic belief in the importance of security and the respect for hard physical labour has collapsed in a policy environment that insists we abandon all resistance to the demands of market forces. Steel must go and tourism must come. Steelworkers should become waiters or social workers. For any enterprise to survive, it must be free to deploy its labour force with untrammelled flexibility. Workers and unions who resist are, by definition, unrealistic, inflexible, or just plain dinosaurs. Concepts of solidarity, egalitarianism and the right to a decent wage simply have no place in the new world of work. A reverence for honest toil is hard to sustain when there is a full-scale war being waged against those toilers' historical rights. Workers are no longer equal parties in the industrial court, with needs that must be defended in the name of a socially and politically defined broader national interest. The interests of capital must be put first or we will all be dragged down by some combination of uncompetitiveness, mediocrity and special pleading. And these are claims that no amount of empirical disputation seems to dent.[29]

Not only has the working class had much of its blue-collar employment removed, but it has also been deprived of the respect for honest toil that went with it. Honest toil is a concept that has been politically hijacked and used to construct a quite different kind of moral framework. It is now, it seems, something that only the self-employed and small businesses can really understand—the new battlers—in sharp contrast to the underclass, or losers, whose access to handouts has atrophied their ability to get up and go.

There is a disturbing common theme in the diagnoses of what ails the underclass—the notion that it is attitudinal problems that prevent welfare recipients from getting off welfare.[30] At its most charitable, it is argued that long periods of welfare dependency, resulting from long-term unemployment or lengthy periods of full-time parenting, for example, erode people's ability to see and take advantage of the opportunities for economic independence that do exist. Indeed, they erode their capacity to participate economically and socially more generally. The fact that there is no evidence to suggest that the underclass are any different from anyone else in their patterns of social participation seems irrelevant to this ideological debate.[31]

This framing of the problem encourages us to believe that this part of the underclass needs firmness, even compulsion, in its own best interests. It needs to be 'obliged' to stop being a drain on all of us. In the charitable version there is an acknowledgment that the vision of converting the welfare-dependent into self-employed or employees could cost a lot of money, but there is no discussion of where this money might come from. This is hardly surprising, since anyone of any influence has been convincing us for far too long that high taxes and other forms of income redistribution are bad for the economy.

The uncharitable versions, which have always emanated from what used to be called the petty bourgeoisie—the owners of fish and chip shops, for example—see the culture of welfare dependency as a culture of laziness and special pleading and welfare recipients as people who simply need to be made to realise that the handouts are finished.[32]

The charitable and uncharitable versions resonate together partly because of the history of class interests in Australia and our 'residual' welfare state that has always relied on paid work as the fundamental source of income security. What all versions fail to acknowledge is that there are not enough jobs and that making the most vulnerable compete more strenuously simply jeopardises the minimal security experienced by the other half of the new underclass—the precariously employed—and, increasingly, the security of the working class. Yet all parties are arguing for a more selective, more conditional, more judgmental, less 'generous' and more paternalistic welfare system. We have returned to that old practice of dividing the underclass into the deserving poor and the undeserving poor.

And maybe we can't any longer assume that we know how to provide enough jobs as the basis of income security for all?[33] If that is the case we face an enormous challenge in rethinking the foundations of economic security for the underclass and the more vulnerable sections of the working class. Every plausible solution to the problems of growing inequality and detachment or marginalisation requires considerably higher levels of taxation. Here in Australia we have no shared historical policy framework for such actively redistributive measures, despite our long history of egalitarian sentiments.[34] This is not to say that we cannot develop such a framework, for there is no logical contradiction between an open and internationally competitive economy and the welfare state.[35] But redistributive measures have to be funded out of taxes on incomes and sales. As a recent analysis of globalisation and welfare puts it:

> This means that the public must both want welfare services and be willing to pay for them. It implies both solidaristic values and appropriate political institutions that force decision-makers to respond to those values. Hence both attitudes and institutions become central, in the form of distinct national legacies that favour solidarism and public consumption. Societies without such inheritances or the means to invent them will thus feel the pressure.[36]

For much of the century since Federation, Australian attitudes and institutions combined to mediate class relations within a framework that acknowledged social values and egalitarian manners. The institutions have been seriously undermined as class interests have diverged and new class interests have found themselves unrepresented. Resistance to class power has been fragmented so that resistance itself looks chaotic.

Despite the challenges posed by the dramatic economic changes of the last twenty years, we are a richer country than ever before. The problem is that far too many people have been excluded from the benefits. As long as the overclass insist on arguing that we cannot have economic growth *and* social welfare, there will be a space for One Nation and the politics of grievance. In the politics of grievance, those who work very hard but have increasingly little to show for it start to blame anyone who doesn't work (whether it's their fault or not) and anyone who might be seen to be taking Australian jobs—which puts Aboriginal people, single mothers, the unemployed and Asian migrants in the frame.

Conclusion

If we want to be able to go on sitting in the front seat of the taxi and talking respectfully with each other across class differences, we must first of all face up to the scale and depth of the social and economic marginalisation that we have allowed to occur in recent years and the intensity of people's feelings of insecurity. If we want to revive egalitarian manners we must engage in a mutually reinforcing process of mobilising our egalitarian traditions and building new institutions that regulate the market and redistribute the wealth it creates. The possibility of political solidarity between the middle class, the working class and the underclass—I don't think I'd count on the overclass—depends, in part, on our ability to remember and revivify an emotional solidarity that is there in our history.

Endnotes

1. These examples are all taken from R.W. Connell, 'Images of Australia', in *Social Change in Australia*, ed. Donald E. Edgar, Cheshire, Melbourne, 1974.
2. D.H. Lawrence, *Kangaroo*, Penguin Books, Harmondsworth, 1989, pp. 11–15.
3. John Murphy, *Imagining the Fifties*, University of New South Wales and Pluto Press, Sydney, 2000, p. 145.
4. Craig McGregor, *Class in Australia*, Chapter 7, 'Who is the middle class?' Penguin Books, Ringwood, 1997.
5. Quoted in Ian Marsh, *Beyond the Two Party System*, Cambridge University Press, Melbourne, 1995, p. 26.
6. John Rickard, *Class and Politics*, ANU Press, Canberra, 1976, pp. 1, 288.
7. ibid., p. 286.

8. Murphy, op. cit., pp. 81–90.
9. Don Aitkin, *Stability and Change in Australian Politics*, ANU Press, Canberra, 1977.
10. David Kemp, *Society and Electoral Behaviour in Australia*, University of Queensland Press, St Lucia, 1978.
11. Constance Lever Tracy & Michael Quinlan, *A Divided Working Class*, Routledge and Kegan Paul, London, 1988.
12. Quoted in 'You have to go to Melbourne if you want a good job' by Anna Bodi, Glenn Maggs & Joanna Gray, Centre for Workplace Culture Change, RMIT, Melbourne, 1998.
13. Peter Saunders, 'Income and Welfare', in *2001 Year Book Australia*, Australian Bureau of Statistics, Canberra, 2001.
14. This is the term used by Guy Standing in his *Global Labour Flexibility: Seeking Redistributive Justice*, Macmillan, Basingstoke, 1999.
15. ACIRRT, *Australia at Work*, Prentice Hall, Sydney, 1999, p. 95.
16. ibid., p. 42.
17. ibid., p. 61.
18. ibid, p. 67.
19. Department of Employment, Education and Training (DEET), *Australia's Workforce in 2005: Jobs in the Future*, AGPS, Canberra, 1995, pp. 43–4.
20. Robert Reich, *The Wealth of Nations*, Vintage, New York, 1992.
21. An illuminating concept used by James Gee, Glynda Hall & Colin Lankshear in *The New Work Order: Behind the Legend of the New Capitalism*, Allen and Unwin, Sydney, 1996.
22. This figure excludes Catholic schools where the figure is about 75 per cent. See Dusseldorp Skills Forum, *Australia's Youth: Reality and Risk*, DSF, Sydney, 1998, p. 54.
23. DEET, op. cit., p. 33.
24. Liz Porter, 'Our working poor', *Sunday Age*, 11 March 2001, p. 6.

25. Senator Jocelyn Newman, 'Discussion paper: The challenge of welfare dependency in the 21st century', Department of Family and Community Services, Canberra, 1999.
26. Iain Campbell has provided a range of indicators for Australia. See his 'Beyond unemployment: the challenge of increased precarious employment', *Just Policy*, no. 11, December 1997; ACIRRT, op. cit., Chapter 6, 'Job security in a changing labour market'.
27. There is no evidence that work-poor households suffer from a culture of dependency as opposed to a shared lack of objective opportunities for unskilled employment. See Bruce Bradbury, 'Added, subtracted or just different: why do the wives of unemployed men have such low employment rates?' *Australian Bulletin of Labour*, vol. 21, no. 1, 1995, 48–70.
28. Newman, op. cit., p. 4.
29. P. Boreham, G. Dow & M. Leet, *Room to Manoeuvre: The Politics of Full Employment*, Melbourne University Press, Melbourne, 1999; Stephen Bell (ed.), *The Unemployment Crisis in Australia*, Cambridge University Press, Melbourne, 2000.
30. See my 'The McClure Report on welfare reform: policy debate in an election year', in *Australian Options*, 2001.
31. See Appendix 3, 'Patterns of income support receipt and reliance', in the Technical and Other Appendices to the *Interim Report of the Reference Group on Welfare Reform*, Department of Family and Community Services, Canberra, March 2000, p. 32.
32. See Judith Brett, 'John Howard, Pauline Hanson and the politics of grievance', in *The Resurgence of Racism*, eds Geoffrey Gray & Christine Winter, Monash Publications in History 24, Clayton, 1997.
33. See Standing, op. cit., for the argument that this is probably the case, and Bell, op. cit., for a public sector employment solution to this problem.

34. Bell, op. cit., p. 267.
35. See Paul Hirst & Grahame Thompson, *Globalization in Question*, 2nd edn, Polity Press, Cambridge, 1999, Chapter 6: 'Can the welfare state survive globalisation?'
36. Hirst & Thompson, op. cit., p. 166.

Rick Farley

The cities or the bush: Is that the real problem?

I acknowledge the Wiradjiri people, the traditional Aboriginal owners of the lands where we meet, and offer my respect to their elders and to their living culture.

Australia's Aboriginal culture is the oldest surviving culture in the world. I would like to borrow from it and tell you my story so you have a context in which to judge my comments today.

I was born in north Queensland, where the closest capital city is Port Moresby. I went to school and university in Brisbane, which is as far from Cairns as it is from Melbourne. My degree is in drama and literature, which no doubt was of some help later on the political stage.

I was a city boy—at least insofar as Brisbane qualified as a city in the 1960s. Many would argue that it did not achieve such status until after the Commonwealth Games and Expo. My father died when I was young and my mother worked to ensure my sister and I attended private schools. She believed that a good school (not only a good education) was essential to our future prospects. Ours was not an affluent household.

My university days were coloured by 1960s 'flower power', a lot of heady but ultimately impractical debate, theatre and some radicalism—the Springbok demonstrations, anti-Vietnam marches. In those days, young people still believed it was possible to change the world.

After I graduated, I moved to Nimbin for the Aquarius Festival—Australia's answer to Woodstock—and enjoyed being a hippie for a while. I sometimes still wonder what I'm going to do when I grow up.

In 1974 I moved to Rockhampton, became a journalist on the local newspaper, and ended up on the staff of a minister in the Whitlam government. I helped set up a Labor government public relations machine to take on Queensland's Bjelke-Petersen government.

The Cattlemen's Union was formed in 1976 as a breakaway from the established Graziers' Association. They wanted a PR operation and offered me a job. Whitlam had been sacked, I was at a loose end and so I took the job. That changed my life. It started my apprenticeship in rural politics, one, I may say, that has never ended. I worked for the Cattlemen's Union for ten years and became its executive director at the age of twenty-six—with my liberal arts, hippie, ALP background. They were brave men, those leaders of the Cattlemen's Union.

I went from Rockhampton to the National Farmers' Federation (NFF) in Canberra for another ten years and was executive director for seven of them. Some people thought I was 'the leftie from the right'.

During my twenty years with farming organisations, I saw and learned a lot. I saw the face of rural poverty up close—stalwart families who opened up brigalow blocks with minimal capital only to see beef markets collapse when Japan closed its markets after the oil shock. Many were living in tin sheds with earth floors, young kids and a car seat for a lounge. Not the common view of a pastoralist.

I saw the class differences and bitter splits between the established graziers—mostly woolgrowers and the large cattle companies—and the farmers and small cattlemen. Part of the folklore was that you could always tell the difference between a grazier and lesser mortals by their boots. Graziers had leather soles because they never got off their horses.

I saw fierce internal farm sector debates about protection and tariffs. In general, those industries operating on the domestic market wanted some protection, while exporters, who paid for it, wanted protection reduced. Every farmer wanted a more flexible labour market.

I saw the sector come to understand and accept that protection was the trade-off for centralised wage-fixing. If there was to be more competition in the labour market, there had to be more competition in product markets. Two of the pillars of the post-Federation 'Deakinite settlement' to which Paul Kelly refers in *The End of Certainty*[1] had to be dismantled together.

I saw the pain that goes with industry deregulation—in the sugar industry, the dairy industry, the grains industry, the citrus industry and finally in the wool industry. Many people went broke, empires collapsed and the social structure of rural and regional Australia changed enormously.

I saw industries grapple with the impact of changing from a fixed to a floating exchange rate and the rapid development of a much more international market place, propelled by the communications revolution. More people got left behind, not only in the regions but throughout the national community.

I saw the costs of environmental degradation hit home. The farm sector started to calculate losses in potential production and to focus on the need for more sustainable management of natural resources. That prompted the historic negotiations between the NFF and the Australian Conservation Foundation, which led to the national Landcare program and the Decade of Landcare. It also generated even more pressure for changes in enterprise management.

I saw the Mabo judgment and the legal reality of native title—another major and long-overdue change in the nature of relationships in rural and regional Australia.

I left the NFF in 1995. Since then, I have shifted from the macro to the micro, from the somewhat rarefied heights of national policy to trying to achieve change at local level. I now work in the area of land use agreements, where industry needs to accommodate native title rights and environmental safeguards. It is very different from what I used to do.

For the last ten years I have been heavily involved in the reconciliation movement because there is no other choice about race relations that is acceptable to me. I have seen the generosity of Indigenous people as they continue to offer us the gift of their culture while every day they feel the deep pain of social injustices that shame us all.

It is my honour to present one of the Barton Lectures as part of the centenary of Federation. I am not an historian, not even an academic. All I can do is share with you some of the understandings I have reached from my range of experiences. I cannot speak for other people and therefore speak only for myself.

The cities or the bush—is that the real problem? I don't think so. I think the real issue is how Australia manages the forces of inevitable and ever faster change. There are problems that are common to the capital cities, regional cities and rural areas. They no doubt will have new prominence in the wake of the 2001 Western Australian and Queensland elections, but they have been around since Federation, although more acutely since the big economic decisions of the 1980s.

I shall begin by reminding you that the three practical forces that shape our communities are the interrelated forces of landscape, employment and population.

First, the landscape helps to shape our communities. The saltwater people are different from the desert people. Water catchments define regions of common interest because water is the most precious commodity in the driest continent on earth except Antarctica. Two-thirds of our country is arid or semi-arid. The most hospitable country, where there is relatively secure rainfall, is on the east coast and in the south-east and south-west corners of the continent. That will always be where most people want to live.

Second, since Federation there has been a major shift in employment away from primary industries and manufacturing towards service industries. Primary and manufacturing industries' share of employment has fallen over the century from more than 50 per cent to about 18 per cent today. Services now account for over 80 per cent of total employment. That, too, has shaped our communities.

Service industries need population to be concentrated and employment has been falling in rural areas.

Third, as a result of those landscape and employment pressures, population has shifted over the century to larger centres and towards the coast, where it is most attractive to live. At the time of Federation, almost half the population lived in communities of fewer than 3000 people and 40 per cent lived in rural areas. By 1996 only 18 per cent lived in these small communities and only 15 per cent lived in rural areas. More than 80 per cent lived within fifty kilometres of the coast.

The capital cities have always accounted for a huge slice of the population, but regional cities have also grown substantially since Federation. Indigenous people are becoming a bigger part of remote communities. Australia's national identity is now more about the beach than the bush.

The social structure of rural and regional Australia therefore has been undergoing profound change over the century. Population has shifted and concentrated, reflecting employment opportunities, and infrastructure has followed. Middle-sized family farming enterprises are under the most pressure. They are either being amalgamated for economies of scale or carved up as hobby farms around regional cities.

In January 2001 the *Australian* newspaper carried a feature article 'Bitter harvest burns sugar', dealing with the problems encountered by the small South Johnstone sugar mill in north Queensland as it attempted to adjust to world markets. It had gone into receivership owing $25 million. Just two weeks later in the same newspaper, there was another feature article that quoted Janet Holmes à Court: 'Everyone in farming in Australia realises it's a new ball game. It's not all about hands in the dirt, it's about hands on the computer. It's not about talking to your bank manager—most have disappeared. It's about talking to your rural adviser and scientific adviser.' The same article reported that the Stanbroke Pastoral Company, the largesst landholder in Australia and the biggest cattle producer, was well down the road to vertical integration, owning its own feedlots and abattoirs. Kerry Packer's catte company Consolidated Pastoral Company was also reported as vertically integrated, with its own breeding, fattening and abattoir operations.

That's the changing face of rural and regional Australia. The ruling equation is how best to operate in the international market place. If you can't get better or get bigger, get out.

And there is no going back. Our nation is simply too small to stand apart from the rest of the world. While we have a population of twenty million people, we have a small domestic market, so our companies must export in order to grow. Our small population also translates into a small tax base, so the levels of support and assistance available from our government are much lower than those available to countries with large populations.

The major economic decisions of the 1980s—to float the Australian dollar, deregulate financial markets, reduce industry protection and free up the labour market—were inevitable and they are irrevocable. They recognised finally that Australia had no option but to become part of the growing international market place.

Change has always occurred in Australian society, but the pace is now accelerating. The competitive environment in which Australia has to operate is evolving ever more rapidly. As has been noted: 'Thirty years ago, knowledge doubled every fourteen years—it is now doubling every seven years. Not only is the speed of discovery increasing, but the rate at which knowledge is applied has also become more rapid.'[2]

As change continues to accelerate, groups in the community have been left behind, and not only in rural areas. They are concentrated around primary and manufacturing industries, where employment has fallen in relative terms.

In my view there is a community of interests between smaller farmers and those displaced in the restructure of manufacturing industries—between, if you like, elements of the bush and the outer suburbs of the capital cities. Both have been hurt by the pace of change. Both have been unable to find a place in the new international world.

This assessment is shared to some extent by the Business Council of Australia, which has noted: 'In terms of income distribution between 1982 and 1997, every income group has improved its position, with income gains exceeding price increases. In relative terms, the top and bottom of the distribution have done better than the middle.'[3] In other words, the rich are getting richer, the poor are being helped up, and the group in the middle can see the rich getting further away and the poor coming closer.

That is a recipe for frustration, bitterness and anger. I think we are now seeing a new politics of the powerless. Many people in the community believe they have lost control of their lives through no fault of their own, in the whirlpool created by the internationalisation of Australia's economy and markets and the communications revolution. They feel left out, and they want to lash out. In perhaps one of her more intuitive statements, Pauline Hanson has said that she didn't only want to keep the bastards honest, she wanted to get rid of the bastards. She is a touchstone for the politics of the powerless because they know they can't change things, they just want revenge.

I believe the real problem is not the cities or the bush. The real issue is how to ensure that as a nation we shape the way in which we have to react to change more effectively and provide equal opportunity to share in its benefits. It's not as simple as the bush versus the cities. The problems are common in the bush, some regional cities and the outer suburbs of the capitals. They have developed over the century, but became much more severe after the big economic decisions of the 1980s, particularly floating the Australian dollar and reducing industry assistance. They were compounded by the mostly *laissez-faire*: 'let the market rule' approach to their social impact adopted by successive governments.

An issue associated with how we manage change is the relative depopulation of the bush over decades. Population has shifted towards the coast, regional cities and the capitals, driven by the landscape and jobs. If Australia wants to change that, landscape and jobs are the keys.

Change affects the entire Australian community and many groups are caught in the fallout. Many would argue that their issues deserve public priority, for example:

- how to give new hope to the youth of the nation and reduce youth suicide and involvement in the criminal justice system;
- a more efficient tax system;
- how to deal with an ageing population;
- funding of private and public education;

- a more efficient health system;
- Indigenous land rights and a treaty.

But in today's political circumstances there is a good chance that the issues of ongoing structural adjustment in the primary and manufacturing industries and the relative depopulation of the inland will receive close attention. That being the case, it is probably helpful to think about an agenda for the process. Others also will have many valuable suggestions.

Sustainable use of natural resources

The first agenda item should be the sustainable management of natural resources. In many ways, it is the defining issue. Care for country is basic to the survival of our entire nation, not just particular sectors. Without more sustainable use of natural resources, the ability of the country to support families and communities will be reduced even further. If we want to improve the long-term survival chances for industry, and therefore our ability to manage change, we have to look after the natural resource base, particularly water.

Our nation is struggling to change land management systems, based on European methods of agriculture that we automatically imported and that are not totally suited to our climate and fragile soils. We have not done a great job up until now.

Land degradation is extensive. In 1999, around 20 per cent of farms experienced some form of land degradation, 16 per cent reported productivity declines and 10 per cent removed land from agricultural production.

Around 2.5 million hectares of land are currently affected by salinity, which in time could rise to over 15 million hectares. Weeds cost more than $3.3 billion in lost production each year.

Nearly 90 per cent of temperate woodlands and mallee have been cleared, resulting in loss of biodiversity. Large-scale clearing continues, particularly in Queensland, despite clear evidence that this increases salinity.

There are increasing concerns about water quality and there is not enough water in some of our river systems to meet the combined demands of agriculture, human consumption and environmental flows.

The cost of arresting these trends is enormous, let alone remedial action. The Murray-Darling Basin Commission says it will be impossible to reverse salinity in some areas of the basin.

If comprehensive action is to be taken, there must be permanent partnerships between landholders and government. Neither can do the job without the other, and it will take a long time. The partnership has to include long-term public funding so landholders have the confidence to change their management practices. That implies the support of all political parties.

The National Farmers' Federation and the Australian Conservation Foundation estimate the cost of necessary work at around $60 billion over ten years. They propose that government meet half the total; the other half would come from landholders and industry.

To build on that proposal, Phillip Toyne and I, in a paper for the Australia Institute last year, suggested a 1 per cent tax levy to raise the government's $30 billion. That would be a transparent mechanism to raise public funds in the long term.

I choose to believe that the electorate would support such a levy, providing they were confident it would be used effectively. There are many precedents for a special purpose tax levy, including the Medicare levy.

How we price natural resources deserves very close attention. Until the costs to environmental capital are clearly identified, management of our industries is incomplete. There is no environmental account in the national account. Water is our most precious resource but markets are now inaccurate and incomplete. There are different pricing regimes on different sides of the River Murray. There is no pricing regime on the giant Fitzroy system in the Northern Territory. Emission markets are also not fully developed.

The question then of who pays, once costs are identified, is a separate matter for community and political debate.

Infrastructure

If industries are to compete as successfully as possible on international markets, they must have access to efficient public infrastructure. However, the Institution of Engineers in 1999 expressed considerable concern about this.

The Institution issued a report card in nine categories from national roads to planning. The highest mark was a C. There were five Ds. The Melbourne/Sydney/Brisbane railway system rated F. The report found major problems with the road and rail systems, water supply and sewerage, not just in rural and regional areas but the cities as well.

Clearly, upgrading of national infrastructure is overdue and would have benefits across all industries. Everyone's competitive position would be improved. Rural and regional areas would derive additional benefits to the extent that they are now disadvantaged. To be effective, there would need to be co-operation and integration between all levels of government. National markets offer the greatest efficiencies and strong interlinkages are necessary to develop them. This in turn argues for initiatives to be developed by the Council of Australian Governments (COAG). However, COAG would have to be strengthened, as prime minister John Howard has not relied on it much.

The costs of any such exercise would need to be transparent and taken into account by government and the community. The costs will be high and those with other policy priorities legitimately will want public debate about value for money.

Communications

Equal access to information and service flows is another critical factor in dealing with the relative depopulation of the inland. As markets have internationalised, access to efficient communications has become essential. Without it, industries are at a serious competitive disadvantage.

That is plainly the case in some rural and regional areas where there is no mobile phone coverage and restricted Internet access. In those areas the capacity of businesses to compete is reduced substantially; so is their capacity to protect and create jobs and retain and attract population.

Adjustment

Adjustment packages can then be targeted to industries and regions experiencing particular difficulties. Regions can also be targeted for special development. There are many such examples since Federation—motor vehicle plans, steel plans, the brigalow schemes, Albury/Wodonga and so on. The packages can include such things as access to discounted capital, tax incentives, education and training, provision of infrastructure and research and planning.

Elements of the primary and manufacturing industries have a legitimate case for special adjustment assistance. They were left largely to fend for themselves after Australia's markets were opened in the mid 1980s. The social impact of change was managed woefully by government in many areas. Their position now raises important national issues, not least the relative depopulation of the inland.

If the issues are to be addressed, once again an integrated approach by all levels of government would deliver the most benefits. The Commonwealth, states and local government all have programs that could be applied. COAG again would be the most logical vehicle and particular regions could be targeted according to an assessment of needs.

For this to occur, the national community would need to agree to give priority, both political and economic, to the problems of the primary and manufacturing industries and to some regions of Australia. There would need to be a national debate where those with other priorities could put their case. Costs would need to be understood clearly. Government should be prepared to proceed only where there is a clear mandate for action. The support of all political parties would be necessary because programs would have to extend well beyond the normal budget process.

Local ownership and delivery

From the most recent state elections and public opinion surveys, we know that a lot of people feel disconnected from governments and public institutions and absolutely frustrated about their ability to control their lives. We also know that the most effective government programs are those that reflect the priorities of the local community and that are owned by the community.

The concept of giving communities some control of government programs in their region should therefore have some attraction. It could serve both to engage those who now feel shut out and improve the ownership and effectiveness of the outcomes.

Noel Pearson is discussing an exercise like this with Queensland's ALP government on behalf of Aboriginal communities on Cape York. He calls it the 'Partnership Program'. The principle is to regionalise program administration, identify all the ways government is dealing with the community and give the community some say in priorities and how the programs are delivered.

Regional administration and delivery of programs by all levels of government, with some community control, certainly appears worthy of further discussion. Water catchments can help define natural regional boundaries. It would have the added dimension of government and public institutions being seen to reach out for the disaffected in the community and trying to heal divisions that clearly exist.

Once again, it would be logical to approach such an exercise through COAG because all levels of government have some programs in the same areas.

At the end of the day, when everyone else has packed up and gone home, it is the people in the community who have to live next door to each other and deal with each other. If they are not happy with the outcomes, there will be no final resolution of the issues and government and politicians will continue to have a big problem.

Native title

My experience has been that after some initial hysteria, developers are learning how to deal with native title, although with some extra costs. Indigenous communities are not opposed to development—in many cases, it gives them their only chance to develop their own economic base.

Companies have developed new skills, just as they had to do for environmental assessments. Their preferred approach usually is to reach an agreement with traditional owners, recognising that they have the same community obligations to Indigenous people as they do to other groups. In a more pragmatic sense, they also recognise that it is better to front-end load their risk and devote some resources to negotiated outcomes in the first instance rather than face the prospect of litigation over the life of their project. This is particularly the case where companies expect to do repeat business with Indigenous communities.

The desire of companies to reach legal agreements about native title now generally exceeds the capacity of traditional owners to respond, because:

- traditional boundaries have become blurred by dispossession, so identifying the native title group often is difficult;
- genealogical research has not been completed before many native title applications are lodged, so defining the native title group also is difficult:
- native title representative bodies are not in a position to devote significant resources to agreements. Their main priority is test cases to extend the law;
- many Indigenous communities do not have corporations that can deal commercially with developers and government and that can hold native title rights and interests.

Government also has its own gaps to fill on native title. Some states still have not fully resolved the evidence they require before accepting groups as legitimate claimants for the purposes of an agreement. Some still have to develop efficient protocols between their agencies to consider and sign off on agreements.

Negotiated outcomes about land use are obviously the best result for everyone. There is community ownership of the results, costs are reduced and the benefits of development are shared. It would therefore be sensible to devote greater public resources to facilitating native title agreements. Native title is clearly a factor in managing change in many inland areas.

Looking forward

The most important step would be for everyone to look forward. Mistakes have certainly been made in the past, but they are in the past. The most relevant question is what should be done to fix them, so work can begin on a forward agenda.

The politics of revenge can go only so far. Eventually, people have to roll up their sleeves and get on with the real job, which is to find some solutions. There really is no other alternative. Internationalisation of trade, capital and information will continue. Australia can't stop it and we are too small to remain as an isolated fortress economy. Change will occur faster and faster—consider the recent breakthroughs in gene mapping and the possibilities they raise. Australia has no option but to swim in the international whirlpool and our industries must continue to adjust.

The issues are tremendously complex. Many of them have been around since Federation. The shifts in employment and population have certainly occurred over many years. The accelerated pace of change since the big economic decisions of the 1980s has brought many issues to a head. Because social impact has been dealt with poorly, there has been a loss of public faith in the central institutions of society: 'Just get rid of the bastards'.

Part of the challenge is to provide the leadership and vision necesary to chart these waters. Leadership needs to be at many levels—certainly from the prime minister and premiers but also in the regions, from business, trade unions, Indigenous people and learning institutions.

A co-ordinated national effort in which everyone looks forward would be in Australia's best interests. We have few enough resources as it is. It makes no sense for our communities to diminish our potential national effort by indulging in vendettas.

The tasks would be easier if there was a set four-year term of federal government. The current arrangements limit the viability of long-term initiatives to address structural change. The benefits don't necessarily emerge during what is effectively a two-year political cycle and it is difficult to achieve a bipartisan approach to major issues. There is more opportunity to shape the impact of change where the term of government is longer. Some of the states already have four-year fixed terms, so there are working precedents for the Commonwealth parliament.

In conclusion, I think the value of the centenary of Federation is the opportunity it provides to reflect on our history and where we go from here. I sincerely hope that opportunity is not bypassed and wasted. There are many important issues for Australians to consider.

'The cities or the bush' is not the real problem. The core issue is how we all shape and manage the impact of change and internationalisation on our communities.

Conclusion

Change has been occurring throughout the century. At the time of Federation almost half our population lived in small communities. Many of them have disappeared over time. It is not a new trend. Population has moved consistently to regional cities, the capitals and towards the coast. More than 80 per cent of the nation now lives within fifty kilometres of the coast.

Population has shifted in response to landscape and job pressures. Primary and manufacturing industries have declined in relative importance since the mid twentieth century and service and information industries have grown. The new growth industries are based in population centres, particularly along the coast where rainfall is more reliable and the country is most hospitable.

Government has managed the social impact of the big economic decisions of the 1980s very poorly. As one result, some elements of primary and manufacturing industries have not been able to adjust fully, and their share of national wealth has been reduced.

They tend to be in particular regions, so the impact is not spread evenly across all regions. They are not confined to rural areas. There are common adjustment issues in the bush, some regional cities and the outer suburbs of the capitals.

Those people have a legitimate gripe. They have been left behind and their predicament raises a lot of very important issues, including relative depopulation of the inland. There are things that can be done to help them—better resource management, infrastructure, communications, adjustment packages. It is possible to provide targeted assistance to particular regions. But for that to occur, there needs to be a national debate about the directions we want to take as a nation, our priorities for political and financial capital. The cost of initiatives for particular regions would need to be identified clearly and interest groups with other priorities should be able to state their case.

However, the issue of sustainable use of natural resources is a stand-alone issue. It should be on every agenda because it is a national priority, as well as one for particular regions. Australia has a unique opportunity to take a holistic approach, as ours is the only continent inhabited by a single nation.

The centenary of Federation provides an opportunity for that sort of debate, but it requires sophistication as a nation. It can only be productive if everyone is prepared to look forward, to concentrate on solutions and outcomes, not revenge. Part of looking forward is to recognise the issues we all have in common rather than concentrating on things that divide us. Every Australian is touched by at least three fundamental issues:

- how we look after our land and waters;
- how Australia shapes its involvement in the international market place;
- how the pain and benefits of change are shared by people and families.

The national spirit in which we all responded to the Olympics, particularly the huge volunteer effort, shows our capacity to pull together.

There clearly are political pressures now for the needs of particular regions to be addressed. The marginal nature of many regional federal seats and the preferential voting system have created a political asset for some. But in my view it would be foolish for politicians to accept automatically that these areas of the community should have public priority. Many want to debate that proposition and they must have the opportunity. Unless they do, the outcomes will be tainted and lack the community mandate essential for long-term structural adjustment.

Leadership is a key ingredient to finding solutions. It needs to come at many levels of our society. Australia is a small nation and cannot afford the indulgence of internal division as we try to carve a place for ourselves in the international economy. Neither, it seems, can political parties and partners afford division and instability.

A holistic approach to managing change needs to be developed by government at all levels. Every level of government has a role to play. COAG is the natural vehicle for this process and can be used to a much greater degree.

Finally, though, Australians should think about the soul of our nation. Our future is not just about economics and population trends. The country—the land and waters—sustains us all. If the country is sick, it can't support us as well. If we don't care for it, it can't care for us.

If the country is sick, the soul of our nation is also sad and diminished. Our enthusiasm and energy as a nation fall. Our faith in ourselves and our national confidence are sapped.

I think there are two areas where we can do much more to nourish the core of our national identity. Our land and waters are now badly degraded and we need to manage them much better. The country is sick for that reason.

The country is also sick in its spirit because there are disputes over it. The different interests of the first peoples and those who came later have not been reconciled yet. The first peoples have special rights and interests arising from their unique position. Until they are accepted and respected, the cultural fabric of Australia is incomplete and our soul will stay sick.

So the real problem is not the cities or the bush. The real equation is how the Australian national community manages change, respecting the interests of all groups in our society. We have not been very good at it so far.

We now have another opportunity, offered by the centenary of Federation, to consider what our national directions and priorities should be, and to forge a national effort to achieve them. The nation did that at the time of Federation and it is well past the time to do it again.

ENDNOTES

1. Paul Kelly, *The End of Certainty*, Allen & Unwin, Sydney, 1992.
2. Discussion paper August 2000: Report prepared for Senator the Hon Nick Minchin, Federal Minister for Industry, Science and Resources.
3. Business Council of Australia, 'The shared background', internal discussion paper, February 2001.

4

ELAINE THOMPSON

Challenges to egalitarianism: Diversity or sameness?

Egalitarianism is a word that has been thrown around a lot this centenary year. Our current prime minister has shown a sentimental predilection to asserting the existence of an egalitarian 'fair go' Australian. It's certainly one of the great Australian comfort words. Along with mateship, when we speak of ourselves as egalitarian, we feel positive about ourselves and probably a little self-satisfied.

However we are no longer exactly sure—if we ever were—what we mean when we call ourselves egalitarian. Bob Hawke, prime minister from 1983 to 1991, called on our egalitarian image of ourselves as part of his political persona. Hawke attempted to personify this sort of Australianness; his drinking record and his sexual chauvinism identified him as an archetypical Australian; his accent, despite an English postgraduate education, remained intractably and enthusiastically broad. Hawke's style clearly met with the approval of mass Australia. As the silver-haired larrikin, the silver bodgie turned mostly respectable, Hawke was popular, even when his political party and policies were not.

Of course Hawke was not really our egalitarian folk hero. Unlike Bob Hawke, our folk hero was usually a battler. I suppose Crocodile Dundee and the hero from 'Seachange' represent the old egalitarian view of ourselves. Here we have the easygoing, irreverent Australians who are intimidated by no one, judge people on their merits and treat everyone equally. This character has been with us a long time and is part of our folk stories. He is the drover, the Man from Snowy River, the cane cutter in *The Summer of the Seventeenth Doll*, the digger.

He was never the boofhead of so many Australian television ads or the fool of a father in the movie *The Castle*. Our folk hero—and he is always male—had failings, especially in that he was sexist in the sense of being uncomfortable in the company of women. Some have accused him of being, at the psychic level 'homosexual', bonding to his male mates far better than to his often neglected wife. He was usually not formally educated but was deeply perceptive. Interestingly, almost all the male characters in the recent movie *The Dish* have absorbed formal education into the older-style egalitarian character.

Whatever our egalitarian folk hero was, he really is past his time. We still recognise the remnants of an 'egalitarianism of manners', to use historian John Hirst's term, for example, our 'g'day, mate' greeting and in John Howard's oddly inappropriate Akubra hat. But what else?

We still believe that our egalitarianism distinguishes us from other societies. Britain with its class system and the existence of powerful aristocratic self-awareness and a powerful working-class awareness could never be called, or call itself, egalitarian. And it probably would not want to. And I don't think it would ever enter the head of a German or Italian to reach for a term like 'egalitarianism' as a way of capturing a sense of who they are or of what they aspire to.

If I had to pick a single definition of what Americans mean by an egalitarian society, it would be that they are committed to the idea that anyone can get to the top, from log cabin to White House. Bill Clinton has personified this myth, a boy from the poorest circumstances, called 'trailer trash' by his enemies, who became the most popular president in the last fifty years. American egalitarianism does not mean equality of outcomes. Indeed their system glorifies the very differences between individuals, seeing massive economic success in particular as a reflection of America's being the land of opportunity.

Historically Australian egalitarianism, in its image of itself, was very different from that of the United States. There is little agreement on the meaning of equality and what makes for an egalitarian society, for these ideas hold many layers and levels of meaning.

It is hardly surprising then that we in Australia hold multiple meanings for equality and in what we mean by the egalitarian society. Having said that, the idea I want to explore is that at Federation and for most of Australia's history one idea of egalitarianism was stronger than most of the others. Egalitarianism in Australia mostly revolved around the idea of sameness. By and large we believed that all Australians were entitled to a share in the goodies of our society, and that ideally they were entitled to the same share.

This preference for sameness profoundly affected the way we saw ourselves and the way we conducted politics. Over the past thirty years we have attempted to move away from sameness. Our moves have gone in a number of directions. For example, we have become more inclusive and accepted much more social, political and cultural diversity. Those moves away from sameness helped Australia stay unified as it has become a more complex society. If we had not embraced diversity, I think we would be in deep trouble. So the move to diversity was both sensible and realistic.

Over the past twenty years we have also moved away from sameness to ideas that seek to reject equality altogether. These ideas see people as lazy, greedy individuals who need to compete against one another to try and get the biggest slice of the cake for themselves. Such notions are not an accurate picture of the way people are. Certainly people can be greedy and selfish and acquisitive and mean, but people are much more than all that. They can also be generous, creative and altruistic. People don't only seek to maximise their economic well-being; they also fight for ideas such as freedom and the right to produce poetry.

This lecture explores three areas that should give a pretty good indication of how we stand in egalitarian terms. There are many others. However, my three are:

- income and wealth distribution;
- race and ethnicity; and
- voting and our political institutions.

In terms of income and wealth distribution, we are a much less egalitarian society that we once were. We have moved from a fairly benevolent aspiration that sought to ensure that everyone had a reasonable standard of living to a confused set of aspirations largely centred on the idea of survival of the fittest.

In terms of race and ethnicity, our report card is much better. We have moved from an intolerant, xenophobic, socially and culturally rigid homogeneous society to one that has embraced cultural and ethnic diversity, while retaining a very powerful sense of coherence and unity.

Looking at our political institutions, our politicians by and large still behave as they did at the start of the twentieth century and embrace voting as the be-all and end-all of democracy. However, despite the politicians, the Australian people continue to assert their views of what is important. The fact that 25 per cent of us now regularly vote away from the major parties indicates the health of the system, even if it means we have to put up with Pauline Hanson and her ilk.

To take the areas in some more detail, let's start with income and wealth. If I had to choose just one area around which Australians developed their idea of egalitarianism, it would centre on a belief that wealth and income were much more fairly spread in this country than anywhere else. For most of our history, our politicians by and large embraced the aspiration that everyone ought to be able to live a decent life with a decent wage and decent living conditions. That idea was behind our commitment to home ownership and Robert Menzies' dream of a great home-owning democracy. While the reality of wages and living conditions fell short of the aspiration in many ways, at least the aspiration was there—until the 1980s. Since then, and now at the start of the twenty-first century Australia in wealth and income terms is one of the least egalitarian of the first world democracies. Even more important, our politicans no longer aspire to the egalitarian dream.

Let me now explore in more detail this story of wealth, income and egalitarianism.

The gold rushes of the 1850s brought with them the idea that anyone could crack it rich. Moreover, that decade left Australia with the world's highest *per capita* income. Workers' conditions also improved dramatically owing to the scarcity of obtaining labour, and in 1856 the stonemasons' and builders' unions obtained the eight-hour day. The idea of the workers' paradise was born. The decade of the 1870s was described by the *Sydney Morning Herald* as one during which workers were 'the most fortunate, the best paid and the most prosperous in the world'.

Moreover, the fortunes achieved by Australia's wealthiest were lower than those in other developed societies. So it seemed that Australia was egalitarian in the sense that Australia's plutocrats were invisible. The great entrepreneurs and robber barons lived somewhere else—they were overseas.

These figures helped create a sense of well-being and confidence in a people who were few in number and geographically isolated. These are no small matters—egalitarianism has been a powerful force in the politics of Australia.

In relative terms, Australia was a paradise for workers. And Australians looked to government to play an active part in trying to promote our egalitarian dream. In 1904 prime minister Alfred Deakin called on the Arbitration Court to define a decent basic wage—a wage suitable for a living human being, not a cog in a machine—and to define it with the heart, not with an account book. In 1907 Mr Justice Higgins, president of the Commonwealth Court of Conciliation and Arbitration, declared in his Harvester basic wage decision that 'the rate of wages must no longer depend on the "usual, unequal contest" between the employer, who could afford to wait and to choose, and the labourer, who must at all costs win bread'. The standard of 'fair and reasonable' had been interpreted by Higgins as ' "the normal needs of an average employee regarded as a human being in a civilised country" . . . food, shelter, clothing, "frugal comfort", "provision for evil days", a reasonable amount of leisure, security to marry and rear a family of about three children'.

While the Great Depression of the 1930s and the World Wars had shaken a commitment to egalitarianism in terms of wages, the 1950s saw the notion of the egalitarian workers' paradise re-emerge. Jobs were available for the asking, wages were rising, inflation was low and a suburban home was within the grasp of those who put off having children, lived in their parents' garages and saved.

Surveys proclaimed—accurately—that wealth was more evenly distributed in Australia than in any other Western country. Up to the mid 1960s, Australia was more equal in relative income distribution terms than in most OECD countries. In 1973 Australians were told to take pride in the fact that almost all Australian families had some assets, while in the United Kingdom and the United States 20 per cent of families had nothing at all. Similarly the Australian wealthy of that time were less rich than elsewhere. The top 1 per cent controlled 9 per cent of the wealth compared to 26 per cent in the United States and 33 per cent in Britain.

There was, however, a big price that Australians paid for their commitment to egalitarianism in income: spreading a fair and reasonable basic income to so many meant that the rewards for skill were few. By the 1950s Australian skilled workers were paid only 20 to 25 per cent more than unskilled, compared to 30 to 40 per cent in Britain or the United States. And a natural flow-on was that education was undervalued—indeed, treated with hostility and suspicion. For example, until the mid 1960s a university qualified person could still only enter the public service from the bottom through the entrance exam available to everyone. And seniority ensured that there was no fast tracking of the educated. That we have changed from those attitudes in the last twenty-five years has also been a remarkable achievement.

However, we have never been as egalitarian as our view of ourselves. This view claimed that all Australians could share in the benefits of Australia's prosperity. Yet 'all' was defined so that it excluded anyone who was not a white male in full-time work. They were the only ones included in the magic circle of egalitarians. For women, Chinese and Aborigines, egalitarianism was not only irrelevant to their worlds; it enabled their plight to be either ignored or justified.

It took until 1966 for the Commonwealth Conciliation and Arbitration Commission to decide, in the interests of industrial justice, to put Aboriginal pastoral workers on the same pay and conditions as white workers.

Equity in pay for women in general was also steadfastly resisted. The real breakthrough, and the moment when women were finally included into the magic circle of egalitarianism, came in 1974 when the female minimum wage was brought level with the male minimum. However, the under-classification of female jobs was to continue. Today most of the poor in Australia are women.

Perhaps most serious of all, the economic crises that began with the oil crisis in the 1970s were used to restrict the focus of the political agenda to the narrow 'economic' dimension of politics and society. Considerations of economic efficiency and effectiveness meant that Australia retreated from its egalitarian impulses for wage justice and job security.

Despite legislation and government rhetoric about greater representation and equity, the position of most people deteriorated. In both the public and private sectors, people from non-English-speaking backgrounds remained in positions very much lower than their qualifications and length of service warranted. The relative absence of women from the senior echelons of the public service and from memberships of corporate and public sector boards demonstrate the move away from an egalitarianism that earlier reached out to include them. Today Australia is one of the least egalitarian of industrialised nations in the world. The available statistics on the conventional measures of household income reveal that, while income distribution narrowed in Australia for much of the first three-quarters of the twentieth century, incomes have become less equally distributed since then.

Australian Bureau of Statistics (ABS) figures found in the year 2000 that two out of every five families living in poverty had one or both adults working—a stratum of working poor has now been created. And the ABS centenary edition of its *Yearbook* shows Australia as one of the most unequal countries in the Western world. High-income

Australians average more than four times the spending power of lower-income households. And a global study found the gap in after-tax income between high and lower income households was the fourth highest of twenty-one Western countries.

Despite the sentimental commentary coming from our political leaders over the centenary this year, most political rhetoric has changed away from egalitarianism to be replaced by the language of individual acquisitiveness and competition. Social conventions have changed in ways that have made growing income disparities more acceptable. Higgins' dreaming has disappeared.

I believe that most of the people who have voted for the One Nation Party and most of the people who have so loudly repudiated the Liberal/National parties in Queensland, Western Australia and the Northern Territory are also essentially tolerant. For the last twenty years politicians have been talking about competition as if the conditions actually existed for real, open, perfect competition of the market. They've talked of the existence of a level playing field. Of course there is no such thing, especially for rural and regional Australia. Their products have to compete in a subsidised and heavily manipulated world market; the costs they bear in terms of gaining access to almost anything they want are higher than elsewhere; the tyranny of distance still dominates their lives. Most people in rural and regional Australia only want to get what they see as the same share of the economic birthday cake as city dwellers: access to doctors, hospitals, banks, government offices, decent communications, the survival of their communities and, with a bit of luck, jobs for their kids. But they can't get to the cake, let alone get an equal slice.

During the 1990s Paul Keating spoke in parliament of the egalitarian impulse to reach out and give those less well off a helping hand. The then Liberal leader John Hewson countered by arguing that if you reach out to give the less fortunate a helping hand, they will pull you down with them. Government must face up to the challenge from those Australians whose lives have been ruined by the economic changes of the past twenty years. There is nothing wrong with the idea of cross-subsidising different sectors of a society for the benefit of the less well off. Indeed, that is one of the more noble definitions of equality. At the very least our present major political parties should not view the term 'subsidy' as some sort of dirty word that undermines the economy.

Let me now turn to my second area for exploring egalitarianism, that of an egalitarian culture and race.

For most of our history since Federation, tolerance was not a hallmark of Australian egalitarian democracy—sameness was preferred, the 'other' was feared, whether that 'other' involved different ideas, different art or people who looked different. Egalitarianism portrayed Australians as an homogeneous people, whose dominant characteristic was their Britishness. Egalitarianism suppressed and denied the diverse cultural heritage of many Australians. It also created the White Australia Immigration policy.

Several years ago I wrote a book about egalitarianism because I had such difficulty in trying to work out how a society as egalitarian as Australia could be home to the White Australia Policy and also be known for its sexist attitudes to women. How could a society see itself as democratic and egalitarian and be racist, especially towards its own indigenous people and towards Asians?

These contradictions were possible because Australia embraced an idea very popular in European societies around the turn of the twentieth century—the idea of a race hierarchy, with the Europeans at the apex of the human pyramid of civilisations. Accepting this meant that Australians could have a definition of democracy in which only those from what was defined as fully developed human civilisations were allowed into our magic circle of egalitarian democracy. And we could exclude others from that community of egalitarians. The Federation movement was about coming together as a nation, but equally it was about keeping that nation white.

When the national parliament debated the Immigration Restriction Bill in 1901, one member of parliament declared that the coloured races either brought the white race down to their level or, if they raised themselves to the level of the whites, became 'as cunning as foxes, and, notwithstanding our laws and our detective skills, beat us at every turn'.

Those who sought to make Australia an entirely white island believed they were protecting and promoting democracy and used a perverse egalitarian logic to justify their position. They assumed non-white races to be incapable of an equal franchise. The idea of a society of mixed races living on equal terms was never entertained. It was incomprehensible.

At Australia's federation, to profess a commitment to democracy involved a commitment to White Australia. Generally speaking, as the historian Russel Ward argued, 'the more democratic, the more radical, the more "progressive" a person was in other ways, the more strongly racist he was likely to be'.[1]

The Federal Parliamentary Labor Party caucus meeting of 20 May 1901 decided that the first plank of the fighting Labor platform consist of: '1. A White Australia'. The Federation speeches of Alfred Deakin, King O'Malley, William Morris Hughes, Chris Watson and Jim Page all envisaged an Australia where to admit coloured workers meant racial contamination and the creation of 'a piebald people'—a 'Mongrelia'.

Alfred Deakin, Australia's second prime minister, linked White Australia to its material prosperity. Only by remaining white could Australia avoid the anti-egalitarian evil of servility and provide equality of opportunity. Deakin spoke of White Australia as a matter of ethics, rather than economics; it represented 'a principle, not an expediency, a religion, not a view'.

Such a view continued well into the twentieth century. When in the 1920s 'men, money and markets' was the heart of government policy, a best seller, *Australia—White or Yellow?* published in 1926, reminded Australia that it was white men who were sought not only to develop Australia economically, but also to keep it racially pure.

A society of sameness was created where links were made between social homogeneity, homogeneity of values and racial homogeneity. Until World War II the concept of Australian democracy and its egalitarian ways was inextricably linked to the idea of a single race and a single culture.

In the postwar years our massive immigration program was still based on a xenophobic fear of Asia. Immigration and postwar national development were embarked on in order to make Australia strong enough to protect us from the 'yellow peril'. With a breathtakingly innocent capacity to deceive themselves, our politicians justified the mass immigration of people from all over Europe by asserting that through assimilation and integration we could still remain with a single homogeneous culture: that all these new Australians would absorb the British norms of our society and Australia would remain the same. The very term 'New Australian' was specifically selected by the government to underline the sameness of the immigrants. The very positive aspect of this self-deception was that it enabled our political system to increase the numbers of those who were admitted into the magic circle of egalitarians and who could be included within the term 'sameness'. Northern Europeans, Italians, Greeks, people from what was Yugoslavia, Maltese, Spanish, Portuguese, Turkish and South American people were embraced into an ever-expanding definition of 'sameness'. The immigrants were embraced into the circle of egalitarians and entitled to the same share as eveybody else in being part of Australian democracy and in the benefits of that democracy.

Of course we did not remain the same, and our culture was infinitely enriched by the diversity that immigration brought. Moreover, one of Australia's magnificent achievements in the second half of the twentieth century was the move away from an insistence on sameness. We moved beyond the idea that we must be a single race, first to an idea that we must be a single culture, then to a tolerance of diversity. We have made these changes, in the last fifty years with, in relative terms, almost no inter-cultural or inter-racial violence, at least with respect to our immigrants. Unfortunately, our history towards our indigenous people is a very different story. Nonetheless given the ethnic and race-based violence of the last fifty years in

Europe, Asia and Africa in particular, Australia's achievement with respect to its overall cultural tolerance should not be diminished.

So far, despite Hanson and others, and despite the odd repugnant violent acts such as attacks on synagogues, the preachers of race hate have not prospered in modern Australia.

Within my lifetime we have become a changed society. We were a society in which people were ashamed of having an Australian accent. I remember it being a source of pride when I was told that I did not sound like an Australian. We were a society hostile to education. When I started at university there were many circles in which I would not admit to having a university education, let alone becoming an academic with a PhD. We were a xenophobic society. When my mother, a Polish Jew with a heavy accent, first arrived in Australia, she was told to speak proper English or go back to where she came from. When I married at the end of the 1960s I was grateful to be able to take on the name 'Thompson' so that I would not see the glaze of suspicion cross people's eyes when I told them my name, and I would not have to tolerate the sullen hostility from people who would not even attempt to pronounce or spell my name correctly. Perhaps even worse were those who treated me and my mother with ice-cold, rigid politeness. All that has changed.

The third area of this lecture shows a sustained—if a little peculiar—commitment to an egalitarian idea. Because of our commitment to the idea that equality meant that we should aspire to all being the same, Australia's history has, in the main, been one of enthusiasm for a particular form of democracy. To us, by and large, democracy was about equality, and equality involved the ability of ordinary people to vote and to stand for parliament.

The political reforms that took place in the second half of the nineteenth century are clear evidence of an egalitarian dedication to the notion of political equality as opening up the vote.

The Austalian colonies were seen in the second half of the nineteenth century as the 'democratic laboratory' of the world. Between 1852 and the turn of the twentieth century the Australian colonies abolished plural voting; lifted residency restrictions on voter eligibility, allowing large numbers of 'migratory' people such as drovers, shearers, cane-cutters and sailors, to vote; introduced payment for members of parliament, allowing rich and poor alike to stand for election; gave the vote to women; and, at a time when the secret ballot was still being denounced as 'un-English' in England, and called the 'kangaroo ballot' in America, it was the norm in Australia.

The methods through which the federal Constitution was created also centred on voting. In contrast to the American founding fathers, Australia's Federation fathers were no self-appointed lot; they were elected by the Australian people. When a draft of the Constitution had been created, it was sent to the people for their vote and its acceptance rested on success at the ballot box. While it is true that only a fraction of the people actually voted, the basic commitment was to a vote by the people. Australia was unique in that at Federation both its Houses of parliament, were elected—at the time the US Senate was still appointed, and of course the British House of Lords was and remains an appointed, hereditary house.

Egalitarianism in Australia then found its institutional

expression in voting. That expression remains. Australia has more voting systems in operation and has experimented more with different voting systems than any other country. It's as though we believe that if we could get the voting system right, if only the way the voting system worked gave us a fair outcome every time, we could give ourselves a big tick in the democracy column and that would be that; we'd not have to worry about democracy any more. I think that's why we support compulsory voting. At least with compulsory voting, if the voting system is okay, we can know the government we end up with is what most people chose.

We seem to be attached to the belief that the will of the people, as expressed through the polls, was what all that democracy was all about. This view of democracy has given us an addiction to strong majoritarian government. It contains a danger when it comes to minority ideas. In the last decade or so, minority interests have come under attack as somehow representing 'special' vested interests and not representing the Australian mainstream. One hundred years ago, the belief that minority interests ought to be heard, cherished and protected was there (especially with respect to the minority interests of the states) but, even then, it was weaker than the one which held that the majority will, through a strong government elected by the people, ought to dominate. We did not adopt a Bill of Rights. We did not believe that individuals needed protection from government. Rather we had, and still have to a large degree, the view that individual rights may be limited, subject to the will of the majority, as expressed by strong government. Here, then, is one aspect of egalitarianism as sameness: minority views, that is, different views, remain undervalued. Both major parties still fundamentally endorse the strong majoritarian view of government. The compromises they make rarely involve any deeply held commitment to a set of beliefs about the rights of individuals to be different, or the legitimate expression of a different world view—the compromises are made for electoral survival, not for principle.

Luckily Australians are more committed to a vibrant democracy than are our politicians. Politicians may believe they set the political agenda, yet it was the stubborn protests from relatively small groups of people that created the great moves in the agenda over the last forty years— Aboriginal land rights and reconciliation, the women's movement, gay rights, the liberalisation of censorship and the environment are all part of politics because of protest movements, not because of politicians. This vibrancy of debate is what Cardinal Clancy referred to in his speech in April 2001 as the unique aspect of Australian egalitarianism. Maybe he is right.

While I would like to believe Cardinal Clancy is right, what we really have today is a series of cross-cutting ideas about what Australia should look like. Some still yearn for the egalitarian Australia of old; some pretend we are still egalitarian; others wish to drive out the notion entirely and substitute a survival-of-the-fittest view of society justified with words about international standards. Yet others are fighting for a sophisticated multi-layered view, recognising special needs and diversity.

Australia's history up to the 1960s showed a nation insecure about the unknown and hostile to the foreign. Given its past, the remarkable fact today is not how far short of a tolerant, liberal nation we fall, but how far we have come in four decades. Egalitarianism was transformed from a source of intolerance and fear to a liberalising force that advocated the acceptance of differences.

Our main job today is to think much harder to work out what sort of society we want and how we want to divide up the goodies of that society. Egalitarianism in Australia is under siege: the rhetoric of a society of equals has all but disappeared and instead the rhetoric of globalisation seeks to justify a society where competition is a civic virtue and egalitarianism is reduced to a sideshow of Akubra hats and R.M. Williams elastic-sided boots.

The path we are treading is not our comfortable, tried and true path of old. While I certainly do not know exactly what the 'right' path is, the one thing I do know is that the division of the goodies can never be left to the market forces alone.

ENDNOTE

1. Russel Ward, *A Nation for a Continent: The History of Australia 1901–1975*, Heinemann Educational Australia, Richmond, 1988, p. 18.

5

LOIS BRYSON

The new differences between women

Reflecting on the lives of women since Federation I am struck by how much has changed, but at the same time by how much has stayed pretty much the same. Suffragists like Louisa Lawson, who was described as the mother of women's suffrage in New South Wales, as well as being mother of Henry, could rightly feel proud of what has been achieved. In 1888 she started the first Australian magazine for women. She called it *The Dawn* and through its pages declared her vision for Australian women. Its success suggests that many women shared this vision.

The many women's issues that were discussed in the pages of *The Dawn* included the suffrage, conditions of work, unionism, education, equal opportunity in the workforce and the reform of marriage, divorce and property laws. Louisa also advocated building a residential college for women at the University of Sydney. So I am sure she would be keen today to reflect on women's position, but would no doubt be disappointed that many of her dreams took so long to be realised, and that some still remain dreams. Because Louisa was a tenacious fighter for women's employment rights, she would be particularly disappointed that, just as women take up their more equal opportunities the wheels are falling off the employment system and conditions are deteriorating for many workers. And she would be dismayed at the growing gap between those with good jobs, those with bad jobs and particularly those with no jobs.

If we consider change since Louisa Lawson's time, we find most in relation to formal citizenship between women and men. Virtually all the pieces are now in place for equality here, but every day we confront the drag of history. Old ideas about women's and men's roles and ways of behaving still flourish, and get in the way of actually achieving the promise offered by the formal rights. The situation of Aboriginal and Torres Strait Islander women provides a dramatic illustration of the effects of past history.

In terms of the theme of these Barton lectures, unity and diversity in Australia today, the change has provided a far better basis for unity between the sexes now than at Federation. It is, however, women's rights and lives that have been brought more into line with men's. There is far less movement of men's lives towards some middle ground, though there is some. We mostly focus on women's struggle for equality in the public arena and look to the suffragists or the women's movement, but there has also been a subterranean struggle at the face-to-face level. Louisa Lawson and her readers were well aware that the personal is political. Constant concern was expressed in *The Dawn* about 'the man question' and the double standard, about drinking, gambling and violence, and men's sense of entitlement. It was Louisa's mission 'to level men up to the moral standard of women'.

I remember a similar undercurrent in the talk of my female relatives and their friends when I was a child staying with my grandmother in the 1940s and 1950s. They particularly resented the fact that in tight economic times their husbands still felt entitled, as breadwinners, to their beer, cigarettes and a bet or three. At the same time these women were making over hand-me-down clothes, planning cheap meals and earning what they could from the informal economy by the likes of selling eggs or ironing.

As the lives of women and men have moved closer, diversity among women has become more recognisable. I say 'recognisable' because some of this diversity has always been there. There have always been women with disabilities and race, ethnic, religious and class differences, and women have lived in lesbian as well as heterosexual relationships. But many of the differences are in clearer focus in an environment far more attuned to, and more tolerant of difference. This provides a much better basis for unity, because tolerance minimises exclusion.

As well as greater acceptance of the older differences, new differences between women are emerging. These have resulted from the economic, political and social transformations of the late twentieth century, which are continually but far too loosely attributed to globalisation and have resulted in increasing levels of inequality. As Belinda Probert has noted in her Barton Lecture, Australia has gone from being one of the most equal to being one of the most unequal of nations.

New class differences are surfacing just as women take a more active role in shaping their own class position, but inevitably start from very different positions in the hierarchy. Because of the pace of all the change, new differences are also emerging between the generations. The differences between the experiences of young women, women in their middle years and older women have become more marked.

Because I cannot deal comprehensively with a century of change, I want to focus on political citizenship, women's employment, social welfare policy and change within families. I hope this will provide an overview and some insights into why the gender revolution is, as we know only too well, still incomplete.

The vote

Though not actually covered in the Constitution, a Bill passed in 1902 gave white Australian women those two fundamental symbols of citizenship, the right to vote and the right to sit in parliament, though Aboriginal women had to wait until the 1960s for these rights.

Ironically, it was something of an accident that in 1894 South Australian women, including Aboriginal women, had won the right to sit in parliament and to vote. This in turn influenced the Commonwealth to follow suit. What had actually happened in South Australia was that anti-suffragists in the parliament had proposed the right to sit as a spoiler amendment, knowing the government was against it. But such was the momentum that the Bill with the amendment was passed anyway.

Whereas in most countries some women were elected

soon after they gained the right to be, in Australia it took until 1943 before the first women entered the Commonwealth parliament. The first Aboriginal woman was only elected to the WA state seat of Kimberley in 2001. This long journey for Aboriginal Australians provides a powerful illustration that there is not just one history of Australian women, but many.

Even after a century of formal political citizenship, Australian politics remains largely in men's hands. It is encouraging that in a newer, though admittedly less powerful, party like the Democrats many more women are involved and have dominated the leadership. On the other hand it was necessary in the 1990s to establish an organisation, Emily's List, to support Labor women's election campaigns.

Employment

When we turn to employment, we find that the policies framed around the time of Federation and now referred to as the 'Australian settlement', had a strong masculine bias that continues to affect women's lives. The legacy of the settlement's racist bias remains as well. In my reading, the two elements that most impinged on women's rights were the defining of women as dependents of male breadwinners and the systematic attempt to minimise women's capacity to compete with men in the workforce.

Over most of the nineteenth century, government statistics had counted most women as economically active, effectively co-breadwinners. But at the turn of the twentieth century, partnered women's household contributions were redefined as non-economic and expunged from the national accounts. Only very recently has consideration been given to how national accounting systems may reinstate the value of the huge amount of unpaid work that is done mainly by women.

Also around Federation male unionists gained a family wage, meant to support a man, his wife and his three children. Unique to Australia and New Zealand, this was a ground-breaking social experiment. It established a white male wage earners' welfare state on the basis of a guarantee of a family's economic well-being, through a minimum male wage set by regulation and struck at a level judged to be adequate rather than being set by employers. All employed white men were entitled to it, whether they had a family or not. But women workers received only 50 per cent of the rate, even when they were sole breadwinners. The family wage was finally abandoned in 1974 as the last part in the establishment of formal equal pay for women.

The wage earners' welfare state did deliver to most Australian families a reasonable standard of living, with less income inequality than in most other countries. However, this favourable assessment of Australian inequality relies on treating the family as a unit and assuming that income is shared equally among its members, a very dubious assumption. Women have remained far poorer than men, something that shows up clearly after divorce.

At the same time as women were being defined as dependants they were being identified as in competition with men for jobs. Unions sought the answer in exclusionary policies, sometimes under the guise of offering protection to women because of their alleged frailty. Louisa Lawson ran into this when she employed an all-female staff to print *The Dawn*. Having refused to allow her workers to join the printers' union, the NSW Trades and Labour Council then called for a general boycott of all printing establishments that employed women. Louisa Lawson wrote in *The Dawn*: 'they have not said "we object to your working because women usually accept low wages and so injure the cause of labour everywhere", they simply object on the selfish grounds to the competition of women at all'.[1]

Women's employment opportunities were systematically restricted and between 1909 and 1912, in New South Wales alone, women were prohibited from taking apprenticeships in more than twenty trades, including baker, butcher, pastrycook and bootmaker. Nor could they become signwriters, paperhangers, tilers, tuck-pointers or undertakers. Some bans were industy-wide, as in the iron trade, while in gilding jewellery women were allowed to work only at the lowest of the six levels. Adrian McGregor, in an article in the *Australian*, points to such actions as part of 'a century of calculated and instinctive discrimination of women by men'.[2]

Other restrictions included the well known ban on married women's employment, lifted in the Victorian public service only in the 1970s. There are many stories to be told here; even my own experiences span many decades. They include my mother's experience in the late 1920s when she had to give up a public service job she loved and was successful at. This rankled all her life, especially because my father, though a gentle, loving person, proud of his wife's abilities, retained the attitude of his time that it would shame him to have an employed wife. My mother eagerly took up teaching in her fifties, fortunately when the family desperately needed the money.

In the 1950s, those days when university students could find summer jobs in factories, I remember my co-workers having to wear their wedding rings on strings around their necks while at work. Then in the 1960s I made the mistake of applying for a public service position, only to have my application returned as ineligible because I was married. In the 1970s my professor at Monash University claimed to a colleague that he had not supported my application for promotion because I was married so didn't need the money, and I would not be able to leave to go to greener pastures. These were also the days when people constantly asked me when I was going to settle down and give up my job.

These restrictions protected men's work, deskilled, devalued and impoverished women, and left many unfulfilled and with few choices other than a partnership with a male breadwinner. They also meant a huge loss of talent that could have contributed to national development.

Since the Whitlam government of the early 1970s women have worked through the state to undo these effects. The same Australian talent for governmental solutions was brought to bear on women's work as underpinned by the innovative, though discriminatory, policies of the Australian settlement. This was another pioneering effort as a cadre of public servants, for whom Australians coined the term 'femocrats', took up the challenge of turning around the disadvantages women had suffered.

The employment regulation structures from 'the settlement' ultimately worked to women's advantage and gains were quickly generalised across the workforce. This has not happened in countries where gains must be fought for on an individual workplace basis. The latter is slow and disadvantages those not strongly unionised. It is dismaying therefore that we are moving towards such a system with enterprise bargaining. Already the gap between women's and men's wages has widened, as have differences between women in strongly and weakly organised sections of the workforce.

The nature of change has been influenced by economic imperatives and an expanding demand for women's labour. Some of this demand is for skilled labour, and the number of women with tertiary education has rapidly expanded. But women are also overrepresented among workers in the new part-time jobs requiring flexible hours and with poor pay and conditions.

Social welfare policy

Australian social welfare policy was very much influenced by the philosophy of the male breadwinner family, but here too women's and men's situations have been brought closer together. This has happened from two directions: women's role as worker has been encouraged and men's role as carer and not just breadwinner has been recognised, though hardly encouraged. Entitlements have been gender-neutralised: those for mothers are now available to parents and those for wives are available to spouses.

In moving women towards the status of worker as well as carer, the national system of child care has been critical. But this is still often seen as a service to mothers rather than to parents, and support for the services remains precarious. Efforts have also been made to move women out of the social security system and into the labour force through more stringent definitions of caring, coupled with encouragement to join the labour market, through training and incentives as well as some systematic pressures. While there are problems with such policies, especially in times of high unemployment, they are part of a process with the potential to promote women's independence. But as with employment, the forces of history mean there are still major differences in the claims men and women actually make on the income security system.

FAMILIES

Families, too, are changing, a fact that excites much public interest. The age at marriage has risen, the number of children has fallen, the rate of divorce has increased, the proportions not marrying and not having children are predicted to rise to over 20 per cent soon, and living together without marriage is a well established pattern. All told, 28 per cent of children are born outside marriage, still lower that the 50 per cent for Scandinavian countries. Women generally are less satisfied with their marriages than men and more likely to initiate divorce.

The capacity for women to survive economically without male economic support has been a fundamental change. This has made feasible the leaving of an unsatisfactory marriage, as well as living without a male partner, though this is still difficult because of women's generally lower earnings. Change has been facilitated by the availability of reliable contraception that allows control of family size and the timing of births. This renders very different the experience of the pre- and post-pill generations.

I remember my mother wishing the contraceptive pill had been available to her. And I also remember returning to the first GP who prescribed the pill for me to ask for a change of brand because the one I had was making me ill. He told me that if I wanted the benefits I had to accept the downside. Fortunately my trusty female chemist came to my rescue with a change of brands.

Similar attitudes survive today, and with serious consequences. This was demonstrated by a young woman from a regional town who is taking part in a research project, called the Women's Health Australia Study, in which I am involved. In 1996 she told us:

> My friends and I went to an all girls Catholic school and out of a graduation of thirty-five girls in 1993, we have sixteen children and I'm only nineteen. This makes me very sad . . . [We] are too scared to ask the family doctor [who] . . . lectures the girls about going on the pill because he is old-fashioned, but the result is pregnancy.

Fortunately not all young women have such experiences, as is made clear by another of the young women in the study who wrote:

> I consider the oral contraceptive pill to be the one discovery which has brought about most change in society. Control in women has changed it all.

Repeated research has shown that the values held about marriage and family have changed greatly, and change is greatest among the young. For example, there is almost universal acceptance that men and women should contribute equally to domestic work and caring and that women have the right to fulfilment from employment and other opportunities. But as with politics, employment and social welfare, reality lags behind. Women continue to do more in the home, and importantly take more responsibility for their families.

How then should we understand this change and the fact that the gender revolution is a global one? Despite all the media talk about globalisation, there is rarely any discussion about what it all means for women. German sociologist Ulrich Beck is helpful here because he suggests that globalisation stems from processes of individualisation and this provides a key to women's liberation.[3] Individualisation involves increasingly having to act in terms of what one sees as one's own interests, rather than in a traditional fashion. Beck notes a general movement towards a society based on what he calls 'reflexive modernisation'. He uses the term 'reflexive' to distinguish this phase of modernisation from the earlier phase of industrial modernisation, which we are just moving out of. The new form is reflexive because it involves individuals constantly having to reflect on their lives and choices in an increasing range of areas and with an expanding range of options. Conventional, taken-for-granted ways of behaving are thus challenged as people act more as individuals. Women have much to gain here because their choices have been particularly constrained in the past by their family roles.

To the extent that people really have options—and the poor certainly have few—this opens up wider possibilities. But it also involves its own uncertainties, so much so that Beck also refers to contemporary wealthier societies as risk societies. In practice, decisionmaking is especially complex in areas such as sexual identity, work and family relationships. The new challenges and greater range of experiences lead to new differences between people. This means there is an increasing need for tolerance. It also means recognising that we can only achieve unity through diversity.

Increasing individualisation has destabilised the traditional pattern for women of marrying and having children. I remember noting how taken for granted all this was in the 1960s. Before I had my children, I decided to discuss with friends the pros and cons of such a move. I was met with blank looks and impatience by all but one, who significantly was a social researcher. My question would come as less of a surprise today.

Given the new options, we need to ask: What do women want? In the Women's Health Australia Study we are tracing the health and well-being of three generations of women, young, mid-age and older, over a period of twenty years. All told, about 40,000 women are involved. The 14,000 young women, whose ages then ranged from eighteen to twenty-three years, in 1996 were asked what they want to be doing at the age of thirty-five, and over the years we will watch whether they achieve these aspirations.

At thirty-five, all but 4 per cent want to be partnered and most choose the married option, though 11 per cent indicated the less traditional category 'stable relationship'. Most want children, though 8 per cent said they do not. More than two-thirds want one or two children. Only about one-quarter aspire to a larger family, whereas the study shows 42 per cent of their mothers' and 58 per cent of their grandmothers' generations have had three or more children. Almost all aspire to be employed at thirty-five. Only 4 per cent aspire to the traditional role of being at home full-time. Almost two-thirds indicated they would like to be employed on a full-time basis and almost three-quarters indicated that they aspire to improving their educational qualifications before they are thirty-five.

These findings are in line with other research showing that women are not necessarily choosing radically new lifestyles, but choosing both family and employment, which has become a normalised part of women's lives. Necessity as well as choice enters into this, but then this has always been the case for men too, and it represents a major element in the reduction of difference between men's and women's lives.

The decisions that individuals make about whether or not to have children, and how many, eventually show up in national fertility statistics. And recently we have started to see the outcome of the trend to individualisation. This has caused consternation in some countries, including Italy, Greece, Spain, and Singapore, where fertility rates have fallen dramatically. If the trend in Italy continues, one hundred years hence its population will be only 14 per cent of what it is today. In a group of countries including Australia, Finland and Denmark levels have fallen, but not nearly so dramatically.

The evidence shows that most women in most countries still aspire to have children and that lower fertility levels are a result of not being able to readily combine motherhood with paid employment. Countries with family-friendly employment policies and, crucially, access to childcare have higher fertility rates. It is in countries without such policies that fertility is plummeting.

Let's now turn to where we are at today, and what issues remain to be addressed? Overall there have been far more changes than I can possibly deal with here. Other key issues that have at least partially been addressed straddle arenas as disparate as domestic violence, the right to drink in bars and the right to defend Australia. There has been notable success in education, though some areas with a more masculine ethos, such as engineering and classic blue collar arenas are proving pretty resistant.

A fundamental issue remaining is that value is still defined from a male perspective. It is the classically male roles that still offer more power, more status and greater economic rewards. And virtually all the long-established symbols and icons of Australian society are determinedly masculine and white: explorers, bushmen, bushrangers, Anzacs, sportsmen. These *are* our historic symbols and icons and we must accept them as such, but they should not remain the only symbols. The spectacular and moving opening ceremony at the Olympic Games showed us how these symbols can be used, along with others, in ways that more accurately represent both the unity and the diversity of Australia.

That we haven't eliminated the historic masculine bias focused on competition is well illustrated by Australian parliaments. Certainly there are more female faces but in federal parliament, the one most televised, we still find that so-called debates are aggressively adversarial in tone. Time that should be spent in improving the lives of Australians and promoting the common wealth is spent in ritualised interchanges without purpose, except to maintain or challenge the pecking order.

Also, despite formal equal pay, this remains a crucial issue. Equal value is not recognised and in those occupations concerned with caring and domestic types of services and which are predominantly female, pay rates remain low. In the 1980s, when retraining programs were developed to deal with increasing unemployment among women clothing workers, their skills were found to be close to those of metal machinists. Yet these are mostly males with far better pay and conditions than clothing machinists. But establishing comparable worth has proved difficult. In the 1990s attempts to have nurses' pay levels made comparable to those of ambulance drivers were unsuccessful.

This wages gap between women and men remains not only unjust but also an influential factor in decisions about who does how much paid and unpaid work. While men can generally earn more than women, such decisions are unlikely to be made within families on the basis of equity and choice for either women or men.

This takes us back to the perennial issue of dealing with home and paid work. Most women want a job because it is rewarding, apart from needing the money. But even the mid-age women in the Women's Health Australia Study, whose children at home are older, showed signs of stress in coping with both family and job. However, they generally like being employed and we find that this is associated with better health than not being employed. What is especially bad is wanting a job and not being able to find one.

Among the young women in the study who already have children, we see particular signs of pressure and disadvantage. The average age at which Australian women have their first child is now twenty-nine, among the highest in the world. As more women postpone having children, pursue education and improve their employment prospects, those who have their children young, who also tend to start from a less favourable socioeconomic background, are likely to fall further behind their peers.

All this leads to the perennial issue of the division of household labour, a constant source of tension in many households and an explosive issue to discuss with mixed audiences (and not one likely to promote unity). Nonetheless, as I have suggested, there has been a surprisingly swift change in values about equal sharing in the home over the past two or three decades. As well, in principle, most men seem prepared to do all aspects of domestic work. It is not long since it would have been unacceptable for any fathers to change a nappy, do the shopping and mopping, let alone tuckshop duty, and we can still see these attitudes among some older men. My nephew tells me that when out with his young daughter he has sometimes been accosted by older men and berated for doing what they see as a wife's work.

It has to be faced that feminist activism has been more successful when women's demands have been in line with the growth of capitalism, and less successful in changing behaviour away from the economic and the competitive, towards the more human scale, the supportive, caring and integrative. Essentially women have been enabled to join the workforce, but it remains structured around men. There are only minor, though important, modifications for the different responsibilities that women still have and their diversity. (Even Tennyson observed that 'woman is not uncomplicated man, but diverse', a quote used by Louisa Lawson in *The Dawn*.)

Change in the workplace that should be seen as promoting unity within diversity is often seen as 'just' women's issues, as with childcare, though we now have not only maternity leave but family leave for fathers. But both remain unpaid except for the more privileged workers, and this is likely to continue while the responsibility for substitute wages remains with employers rather than the income security system. Then there is the very serious problem of superannuation, which for many women will not deliver enough income in retirement because their family role has led to interruptions to their employment and to part-time work. This will also exacerbate differences between poorer and richer women.

Given the environment in which women must make decisions about parenthood we can only expect wariness. Not that such wariness is new, as Miles Franklin's classic book, *My Brilliant Career* demonstrates. This was written at the end of the nineteenth century, but the sentiment goes far back in history. Women come closest to equality with men when they do not have family responsibilities, therefore in an individualising society, it can be suggested that falling birth rates effectively represent a baby bust 'we had to have'. Problems of choice are exacerbated by economic insecurity and by the fact that men are not changing their behaviour in the home in line with their new equalitarian values.

The new differences

A by-product of the gender revolution and individualisation has been that other differences between women have more explicitly emerged as women are less constrained by the roles of wife and mothers. Many other differences that were always there we now handle rather better as a nation, though there is a long way to go with indigenous status, race, disability and sexual preference. We need to be still more positive about embracing difference and to make it a lead element for enhancing unity and the common good. In a world with increasing international interaction, the population's multiculural backgrounds are a great asset for diplomatic relations, the arts, the economy, and more. Also with women making up more than half the population, not to more fully utilise and recognise difference and talent doesn't make any sense at all.

Generation differences also add to Australia's diversity today. This has been brought home very clearly through the Women's Health Australia Study. We are finding that the lives of the three generations of women have involved very different experiences, and this means that they face many aspects of life in different ways. Among the generation of young women we find evidence of greater individualisation in, for example, their readiness to carefully assess the medical services they use and state their well informed preferences for change. The older generation is the least critical, while the mid-age fall between. It rather surprised us that it is the young who experience most stress in their lives. Again the mid-age are in the middle and the older women are the least stressed, and indeed are generally active and contented with their lives, though their health is, not surprisingly, not as good as that of the young and mid-age women.

Social researcher Hugh Mackay also found significant generation differences in his study of the baby boom generation, their parents and their children. He sees the differences as being the product of three Australias, not one, and our evidence to date supports this. When contemplating the very different experiences of women over the century, I was reminded of my grandmother who had her eight children during the first two decades after Federation. One of her reflections was on how liberating she found not having to wear long skirts and petticoats, especially for doing physical work, like milking cows and for sport—she was a keen tennis player. What a contrast with beach volleyball!

Where to from here?

During the leadup to Federation and beyond, the shaping of the new nation was an amazing achievement, even though some of the outcomes were unjust. Think what we might do today now that we have equal citizenship rights, have almost escaped the shadow of empire and are much more tolerant of diversity, though issues such as reconciliation mark this as very much a work in progress.

The conversations about women's aspirations for their lives in the new nation were led by suffragists like Louisa Lawson. Women's activism continued, though in a lower key, until it again became very visible in the 1970s and 1980s through the women's movement. While feminist conversations have continued since, they have become somewhat fragmented and specialist. But it is time to again encourage broad-ranging conversations that reimagine gender relations in Australia. We are much better placed than at Federation to make the process inclusive, because of institutions such as Radio National, national newspapers and television and the Internet. This Barton lecture series itself contributes to this task.

The time is auspicious for many reasons. Let me highlight one. Women's role as a dependant of a male breadwinner was essentially a hangover from patriarchal feudal times. With women's lives being modernised we are well placed to take the leap into the future, into Beck's 'reflexive modernity' because women have never become rusted on to the now-passing industrial phase of modernity as men have been. In a post-industrial information age, women's experiences leave us better placed for the task of reshaping the working day, the working week, the working year and the working life, to better meet human needs and take the environment into account. While not necessarily what is best for the twenty-first century, the concept of the six-hour day promoted by earlier feminists does alert us to the need for time for home, community and other activities, as well as for employment. The concept also decentres the economy, making space for other values.

Current family-friendly policies are not likely to be sufficient for the twenty-first century, but clearly change needs to be embraced by governments and employers as well as by individual fathers, men in couple relationships and sons as well as by women. Partners need to take their half share and not just 'help'. Also options that are genuinely 'family-friendly' must not disadvantage with respect to economic, power and status rewards. This essentially also involves a revaluing of a supportive and caring society and a healthy and sustainable environment. Given such change, the next phase of modernity could come close to fulfilling feminist dreams for change. But these are all big asks, though the environmental crisis itself makes serious rethinking essential. Also there are signs that the political arena may be more receptive to such change. The gradual fragmentation of the monopoly of the old political parties and pressure on traditional union structures indicate more ready opportunity for alternative conversations.

If together we can muster the determination and ingenuity evident at Federation, to imagine appropriate collective solutions, we could move towards a reality that much more closely matches our aspirations for equity and unity through diversity. Then we will really be able to achieve the fair and unified society that Australians mythologised in the twentieth century.

ENDNOTES

1. Lawson, Olive, *The First Voice of Australian Feminism: Excerpts from Louisa Lawson's 'The Dawn' 1888–1895*, Simon and Schuster, Sydney, 1990.
2. Supplement: 'The Australian century', *Australian* 17–18 March 2001.
3. Beck, Ulrich, *Risk Society: Towards a New Modernity*, Sage, London, 1992.
  —— 'Living your own life in a runaway world: Individualisation, globalisation and politics', in eds Will Hutton & Anthony Giddens, *On the Edge: Living with Global Capitalism*, Jonathan Cape, London, 2000.

6

JOHN HIRST

More or less diverse

As I was walking up Martin Place, I saw a Vietnamese busker playing a didgeridoo.

My theme is 'Diversity and Unity in modern Australia'. Should the busker be set down under 'Diversity'? Previously buskers in Martin Place were Anglo-Celts; now buskers can come from any nation and race on earth. Or does the busker better belong under 'Unity'? Previously Aborigines played the didgeridoo; now Australians of all sorts play it.

The standard story of what is happening to our society is that it is becoming more diverse. The great migration after World War II broke the unity of the British population of Australia and replaced it with a diverse mix of ethnic groups. At first the official policy was to assimilate these groups into the host culture, into the Australian way of life. Now the policy of multiculturalism welcomes and encourages diversity.

My first message—my quite unsurprising message—is that government policy frequently does not work. What has actually happened during the time of the great migration is very different from what policy intended.

In the 1940s and 1950s the government, supported by its people, did not want migrants to form separate enclaves and perpetuate their own culture and identity. However, this was a free society and its freedoms could not be denied to migrants They did in fact create enclaves; they lived close to each other, opened their own businesses and restaurants and employed their compatriots in them, relaxed in their own clubs, played in their own sporting teams, read newspapers in their own languages; married brides brought out from their home countries. Little Italys and Greek quarters appeared in the capital cities. Suddenly Australia was a very diverse place.

From the 1970s official policy has been multiculturalism. But just as ethnic groups received official recognition and support they began to dissolve; some disappeared altogether. The process of intermarriage between ethnic groups and between them and old Australians proceeded apace. Most of the migrants' children married people who were not of their parents' ethnic group. The rates differed in the different groups. The Greeks showed a strong tendency to marry each other, but by the second generation nearly half of them were marrying 'out'. The Czechs mostly married other people and disappeared.

Most children of non-English-speaking migrants spoke English to each other. If they retained their parents' language, they used it only in addressing their parents or others of the first generation. This was also true of the Greeks, where the retention of language into the second generation was the highest of all ethnic groups. There was also a decline in the Greeks' distinctive religious adherence over the generations. Ninety per cent of the first generation were Orthodox, 82 per cent of the second; 45 per cent of the third.[1]

The territorial base of the 1950 migrant communities disappeared. Migrants prospered and moved from the inner cities to the suburbs, dispersing themselves widely in the process. Their restaurants might continue to operate in their old locations, but if the Italian restaurants in Melbourne's Carlton are still owned by Italians, they do not live above the shop.

Multicultural policy envisaged a world of distinct ethnic groups. This was more and more make-believe. By the late 1980s the demographer Charles Price reported that the Australian population consisted of three groups: 47 per cent British and old Australian, 23 per cent non-English-speaking migrants and their children; and 30 per cent a mixture of the two. The mixture was larger than the migrant group and was set to become the largest group. Price concluded that 'the ethnic character of the Australian population is *not* one where separate ethnic groups live side by side with relatively little social intercouse, constantly perpetuating their own languages and cultures and keeping distinct by continued marriage within the group'.[2]

It should now be obvious that what has happened has not been determined by government policy. In coming to this country, migrants were not encountering a policy but the Australian people, day by day in myriad ways. The outcome of that meeting was determined by the structure, dynamics and culture of the host society and by the composition and aspirations of the migrant population.

Let's look at the migrants first. They came not from one society, but many, and were determined to achieve material success. Because they were strangers in the land, they naturally sought out their own kind and wanted to hold on to traditional ways. But since they also wanted to do well, they had to learn the ways of their new country and adapt to them. They were both assimilationists and multiculturalists.

The migrants were and are in no doubt that there is an Australian way of doing things, an Australian culture. This is the second way that the multicultural label for Australia is misleading. It suggests that there is simply diversity; that there is no dominant culture. Migrants who want to get on and be accepted know better.

In a Nadia Wheatley story, a Greek husband is rejecting a request from his wife that the family acquire a goat: 'A goat, she says . . . And since when did Aussies have goats? Tell me, do you see John Laws with a goat? Or Ned Kelly? Do you think Phar Lap was a goat? In case you haven't noticed, I have a business to run. I can't afford to be a freak'.[3]

More telling is the story of a leader in the Sri Lankan community from *A Change of Skies* by Yasmine Gooneratne. Mr Koyako is worried that the young Sri Lankans in Australia are being lured from their culture. He insists on the observance of the Sri Lankan practice of giving personal names in full. His own name is Mr Mekaboru Kiyanahati Balapan Koyako. Australians, he finds, do not like such long names and he is annoyed that they are always jumbling and shortening them. He decides that Australians are a rude and not very intelligent people.

One day when Mr Koyako visits Yasmine's home Bruce Trevally, an old Australian neighbour, calls by to bring some peaches. Yasmine's husband has to introduce the two men, and of course he must give the Sri Lankan name in full. 'Bruce', he says, 'I'd like you to meet our friend Mr Mekaboru Kiyanahati Balapan Koyako'. 'That's some name you've got, mate', Bruce says admiringly. 'Almost a short story.' Mr Koyako is unused to such directness, but he rallies strongly. To the husband he says, 'Why should you bother your friend with my long name?'. And turning to Bruce he holds out his hand: 'G'day mate', he says, 'Just call me Kojak.'[4]

Let's now look at the host society. In the early critical decades of the migration program the economy was prosperous and expanding rapidly; the trade unions insisted that migrants be paid the going wage rate, and there was easy access to home ownership. If the migrants arrived poor they did not stay poor for long. The society into which they moved was egalitarian in tone, with only a weak status hierarchy and a strong belief that background was irrelevant to social acceptance. Until the 1940s it had been committed to maintaining a white British society, but once the migrants had arrived it was mostly willing to accept them. There was prejudice and resentment, of course, but amazingly little. This is the great Australian success story.

The nature of the society is crucial. Imagine millions of migrants going to a country that cared a lot about who your parents were, or your schooling, or how you spoke, or whether you had read the right books, or whether you gave people their right titles. Australia is the opposite of all this. Because it is easygoing, informal and egalitarian, it was more welcoming to migrants and wanted them to have 'a fair go'.

Another test is to imagine how many other nations would have been instantly ready to bestow their name on foreigners. Arthur Calwell told Australians that they had to call the migrants 'New Australians'. Let's try this style for some other countries. New Japanese? New Germans? New French? New Americans?—maybe. New Britons? Perhaps if they came from the empire, but would 10,000 Italians landing at Dover be called New English? No.

The term 'New Australian' was accepted because Australians did not put a high test on the membership of their community. If the newcomers wanted to make a go of it here and did not make a nuisance of themselves, they could be Australian. The migrants of the 1940s and 1950s were accepted on this one condition: not that they immediately drop their old ways but that they did not parade their differences or transfer their old-world disputes to this new land.

This is a core value of the Australian culture. It's been there almost from the beginning of European settlement; it operated unaltered through the assimilation and multicultural eras. It is not an official policy, but an ingrained belief in ordinary people. It is the belief that there should not be poisonous divisions between people, that this can be a new and better land but only if old-world disputes are kept out of it. The Australian style is to keep differences quarantined and not let them rampage in the world at large.

Of course there have been those who wanted to maintain old-world disputes. The founding European population consisted of three major ethnic groups, the English, Scots and Irish, with plenty of mutual hostility, and these divisions were intensified by the split between Catholic and Protestant. And yet the founding settlers lived among each other; there were no enclaves. The formula for social peace was not to let these differences get out of hand, to find ways of isolating and transcending them. In public life it often looked as if differences had got out of hand, but at a community level polarisation did not occur. This demand not to push old allegiances is still insistent. In the 1950s migrants were told their disputes threatened the Australian way of life. Now they are told their disputes threaten multicultural Australia. It's the same message.

I have been playing down the influence of government policy. It has had its uses. It is best thought of not as controlling events but as reconciling people to change. In the 1940s and 1950s the policy of assimilation reassured old Australians that their world was not going to change, when of course it did. In the 1970s and 1980s the policy of multiculturalism reassured ethnic leaders that their communities and culture were not going to weaken and disappear, when in fact they were.

In the last two decades migration has been occurring in different circumstances. In the 1950s an unskilled migrant speaking no English was at work in a factory the week of his arrival. Now the unskilled work has gone and migrants without skill and the English language remain unemployed for a long time. It may be that we are now witnessing the creation of semi-permanent enclaves in places like Sydney's Cabramatta and Melbourne's Footscray where there are large numbers of Vietnamese. Here unemployed youth and drug taking and trafficking are creating social malaise. Some Vietnamese are doing very well and we are accustomed now to see Vietnamese young people among those who get high academic honours. It may be that the Vietnamese story wil mirror that of the Italians and Greeks and that the early chapters are taking longer to pass.

But I support the decision of the present government to cut back on the family reunion proportion of the migrant intake and to put more emphasis on skilled migration. It does not make sense to bring unskilled people to a country with few unskilled jobs. I am a supporter of a large migration program, but I am not, as you see, one of those who think that once you have started a migration program you can't alter it. We must be free to examine what's happening on the ground and to discuss lowering the numbers and adjusting the mix and even abandoning the program altogether. The attempt to make this topic taboo is a sort of treason against the nation.

I have spoken of an Australian culture and of its being crucial to the success of the migration program. It is ironic then that we now hear proposals that this country can be held together without a distinctive Australian culture, that the concept is outmoded, dangerous and oppressive. Here I part company with Donald Horne, the initiator of this lecture series, and one of the most distinguished advocates of the view that Australia should be held together by a civic faith—tolerance, fairness, a commitment to parliamentary democracy, respect for due process, minority interests and diversity.

Of course I support these civic virtues, but this seems to me a cold and cerebral formula. It does not meet the human need for warmth and belonging. There is nothing distinctive in these virtues. If we were truly a very diverse society with a number of distinct ethnic groups each maintaining its own culture, this is all that we might agree on. But as I have shown, this is not modern Australia.

So here is my answer to the question of this lecture series: How are we to hold together? By being Australian; by celebrating, exploring, criticising and reassessing our Australian heritage, all the things that have defined and still define what it means to be Australian and live in this place. This is not to endorse some noisy nationalism or to insist that we all think of ourselves as bushmen or to promote some bland uniformity. I can best say what I think it does mean by reporting on the work of the Civics Education Group of which I am chair.

This group is in charge of 'Discovering Democracy', the Commonwealth government's civics and citizenship program in schools. The lessons we devised aimed at giving an understanding of our legal and political systems and the opportunities and responsibilities of citizenship. But in addition we included a series of lessons on how Australians have over the years answered two questions: Who is an Australian? What sort of nation is Australia to be?

We have also produced a series of anthologies, two for primary school and two for secondary. We called them Australian Readers. They include stories, poems, songs, speeches and extracts from novels, autobiographies and histories. We encouraged the cultivation of civic understanding and virtue by including Lincoln's Gettysburg address, Martin Luther King's 'I have a dream' speech, Pericles' funeral oration in democratic Athens, Tom Paine on the rights of man, George Orwell on pigs and equality and much more. But we also included Australian material. This is how we sought to feed the imagination of young Australians. We gave them:

- Aboriginal Dreamtime stories
- Henry Lawson's story 'The Drover's Wife' and Russell Drysdale's painting of the same subject
- An account of the Myall Creek massacre
- Albert Facey's telling in *A Fortunate Life* of his epic

journey to escape a tyrannical boss when he was eight years old
- An extract from Douglas Stewart's play *Ned Kelly*
- The convict ballad 'Jim Jones':

> I'll give the law a little shock
> Remember what I say
> They'll yet regret they sent Jim Jones
> In chains to Botany Bay

- Fred McCubbin's painting 'The Pioneers'
- The story of how the penniless Jewish migrant Sidney Myer started his shops
- A Sidney Nolan painting of Burke and Wills on camels
- How Alan Marshall, author of *I Can Jump Puddles*, demanded proper wages though he was on crutches
- How Weary Dunlop stood up to the Japanese and cared for his men
- From Sally Morgan's *My Place*, her grandmother's account of the colour bar in Perth
- The speech written by Don Watson for Paul Keating on the burial of the unknown soldier, the most eloquent honouring of the diggers in our literature.

These readers went to all schools. We did not assume that this material was irrelevant to the children of migrants. We assume that they will be Australians. Of course we included material on migrant experience. The stories of the Greek goat and Sri Lankan naming practices are included in the Australian Readers—as is an account of the journey of a Vietnamese family from re-education camp to what they call freedom in Australia.

I turn now to the division in Australian society that we find most puzzling and disturbing. Over the past fifty years Aboriginal policy has followed a similar course to migrant policy. In the 1940s and 1950s the aim for the Aborigines was that they were to 'live like white Australians do'. The expectation was that the Aborigines would eventually be physically absorbed into the wider population and Aboriginal culture would disappear.

Governments committed themselves to improving Aboriginal housing, health and education. In the 1950s Aborigines were moved from camps and rubbish tips on the edge of country towns to houses within the towns. This policy had only limited success. Aborigines did not like being separated from each other and scattered through the towns; the townspeople were generally hostile.

In the 1970s the policy was abandoned in favour of self-determination. Within a multicultural Australia, Aborigines were to choose how and where they were to live. Governments still spent money on housing, health and education for Aboriginal peoples, but now there was much more spent.

Some of what the assimilationists hoped for has come to pass. Most of the Aborigines now do live in houses, two-thirds of them live in towns and cities, significant numbers are educated and skilled in the Western way, many have intermarried with the wider community. In Aboriginal households, 64 per cent of the couples consist of an Aboriginal and a non-Aboriginal. But with all these changes Aboriginal identity has strengthened and in some places Aboriginal traditional life survives. What would most surprise the assimilationists is that Aboriginal painting, dance and music flourish and have been adopted as part of

Australian culture. Last year at the Federation ceremonies in London a didgeridoo was played in Westminster Abbey. In these respects the policy of self-determination and multiculturalism must be counted a success.

The continuing failure is that large numbers of Aborigines, particularly those in the remote communities, are unhealthy, poorly housed and unemployed. We commonly talk of them as 'disadvantaged'. In talking thus, we assume that they want to play in the same game as ourselves but are being held back; they are handicapped. This is assimilation not as policy, but fantasy. If only there were more funding and less racism, if only the prime minister would apologise and Pauline Hanson disappear, if only there were a treaty, then Aborigines would not live like this.

Consider how they do live on a remote settlement in the Northern Territory where traditional culture is still strong. Here Aborigines marry each other and mostly in the correct skin group.

An Aboriginal family decides it wants to visit Darwin. They do not have much money, certainly not enough for the air fare. They acquire enough for the fare by collecting funds from kin—'humbugging' them is the term. They travel to Darwin. They arrive unannounced at the home of kin, knowing that they will be put up. They may stay some time. If by chance they cannot find a house to take them, they will camp in some park or on the beach.

Here we can see what is called 'disadvantage' at work. The health of these people will suffer through overcrowding—doubling up with kin—or by camping out with no facilities. The education of their children will be disrupted by the trip. The house left empty on the settlement may be vandalised, so on their return the family will have to move in with others and make overcrowding permanent. The people at the settlement, no matter what funds they may acquire, will always be asset-poor because of the claims of kin. Because these people want to live on a remote settlement, few of them will have the chance of getting proper jobs.

But consider the advantages; consider why Aborigines are attached to their way of life. Here are people with few monetary resources who are not tied down. They assume that they can move freely round their realm. They travel without forethought. Saving up and booking ahead are not necesary. Travel, especially travel to funerals, is very important to them. Attending a funeral and the kin and clan business that goes on there for several days is more important than keeping the kids in school or showing up for work.

In these cases the policies of multiculturalism and self-determination are working—Aborigines are choosing to live in a different way—but we don't like the outcome. Nor do Aboriginal leaders like this outcome. They regularly quote damning figures on Aboriginal unemployment, health and housing. It is these figures, too, that attract international attention. They are the political measures of success and failure rather than how rigidly policy adheres to self-determination.

Our concern at Aboriginal health was so great that the federal government in 1995 abandoned the policy of self-determination in an effort to fix it. Responsibility for health was taken from ATSIC, which is elected by Aborigines, and given to the Commonwealth Department of Health.

Here is a great dilemma. Can Aborigines live as other Australians do and yet retain their own culture? There may eventually be a satisfactory accommodation. At the moment it is easy to see the difficulties. Aborigines who believe that road accidents and ill-health may be caused by sorcery will not take the precautions we do. At one settlement in the Northern Territory the clerk told me of two Aboriginal women who were meticulously clean in their work in the health centre; their homes, by contrast, were so filthy that he had to prohibit his children from visiting them. These women knew how to be clean but they did not see cleanliness as relevant to their own lives. It was whitefellas' business.

Of course I have no answer to this dilemma. I would myself not have abandoned the policy of self-determination in regard to health. Aboriginal leaders were among those who urged a Commonwealth takeover. I think they should have been told that if they did not like what ATSIC was doing, they should have worked to fix ATSIC.

If the dilemma is to be solved, it will be by Aborigines. Many of their leaders for the present are pursuing other objectives. Noel Pearson has rightly earned great respect for his decision to return to his own people and attempt to solve the problems they face. He defines the chief problem as welfare dependency. He is working to get proper jobs created in Cape York.

I wish him well. Getting the right sorts of jobs in the right places is not an easy thing. Our political leaders on both sides now say that the market alone should be left to determine these matters. State governments, I notice, still interfere and promise subsidies to business to locate in their territories. If Noel Pearson can find businesses that will locate in Cape York so long as they are subsidised, I hope governments will come to the party. My own view is that sufficient proper jobs cannot be created in the remote settlements and that if all the young are to be employed, they will have to leave. This does not mean that they would cease to regard the traditional lands as home.

There is still huge goodwill towards Aborigines; it is always seeking some new initiative that will settle these difficulties or put us in the way of solving them. The latest project is a treaty.

In Canada, the American colonies and New Zealand, the British made treaties with native people. No treaties were made in Australia and the advocates of a treaty with the Aborigines offer as one of its rationales the need to redress that omission. But a treaty with the Aborigines would not be with a traditional grouping. The traditional groups numbered about five hundred tribes, some of which survive. The Aborigines are a group formed since 1788 from those tribespeople and their descendants who had the common experience of oppression and exclusion at the hand of Europeans. People still living a traditional life do not identify strongly as Aborigines. They are firstly the Gurindiji or the Pitjantjatjara.

The advocates of a treaty are strangely blind to what has recently been done in Australia. We now have a treaty. In 1993, following the Mabo decision of the High Court, the Commonwealth Parliament passed the Native Title Act. This established the procedure by which traditional people can have their native title restored to them; the mechanisms to allow them to manage their lands; the limitations on their disposal; their rights to negotiate with anyone who wants to use them.

This Act was passed after protracted negotiations in

Canberra. An Aboriginal delegation led by Lowitja O'Donoghue, the chair of ATSIC, faced the representatives of the farmers and miners. The prime minister had to get a consensus among these people and then carry it through the Senate that he did not control. Some radical Aborigines were opposed to the compromises necessary to this treaty making and wanted to hold out for something better. Until the last minute it looked as if the two Green senators would back them and stop the passage of the Bill. A way through this labyrinth was found and at midnight on 22 December prime minister Keating was able to report that he had a deal. The Aborigines cheered him.

When I saw photos on the front pages of the newspaper showing the delighted Aboriginal negotiators and Mr Keating, with the prime minister's arm around the shoulder of Lowitja O'Donoghue, I thought: This is the moment of reconciliation, we now have a treaty. Aborigines at last were players at the top table, cutting the best deal they could get with the nation's prime minister. Now I hear on all sides that reconciliation has scarcely begun and that we still don't have a treaty.

As well as the big treaty, a number of mini-treaties are being negotiated across the land. They go under the name of Indigenous Land Use Agreements. These agreements are reached by direct negotiation between native title holders and other users of their land.

Pastoralists are agreeing to allow native title holders access to their leaseholds for hunting and ceremony. Aborigines are agreeing with miners about exploration and the processes to be followed if mining actually begins. When the Mackay Surf Lifesaving Club wanted to build a new clubhouse, the club and the local council negotiated with the native title holders, who yielded control over the site in return for a new park further along the beach.

Treaties with native title holders already exist and more are being negotiated as I speak. Should there, in addition, be a treaty with the Aborigines as a whole? We have already recognised their special position in the nation and the particular problems they face by setting up ATSIC, a unique institution, an Aboriginal parliament within the nation. The Aboriginal and Torres Strait Island Commission, established in 1989, is given funds to spend on Aboriginal advancement.

It is no wonder that those proposing a treaty have some difficulty in saying what it will contain. Perhaps it should declare that Aborigines were the original owners of the land who never agreed to the white occupation? The High Court in its Mabo judgment has already done that.

Some proposals for a treaty seem to me fraught with difficulty and danger. There are suggestions that a treaty should confer particular rights and privileges on Aborigines and provide them with compensation. The immediate difficulty with such a proposal would be to define who the Aborigines are. An official definition already exists. It has three parts. An Aborigine has (1) to be a person of Aboriginal descent, with no particular proportion of this ancestry stipulated (2) to identify as Aboriginal, and (3) to be accepted by other Aborigines as Aboriginal. This definition is appropriately loose. Aboriginal communites in the more settled parts of the country have been very open and accepting.

But this looseness is now being exploited. People are claiming to be Aborigines partly to qualify for the benefits and opportunities specially provided for Aborigines.

Among the deceivers are prisoners in gaols and artists looking for recognition.

Tasmania is the state in which the number of Aborigines is rising most rapidly. Dr Cassandra Pybus, who knows the state and its records well, estimates that three-quarters of the people now identifying as Aborigines do not have an Aboriginal ancestor.

In 1997 Michael Mansell, the Aboriginal leader in Tasmania, brought an action in the federal court to challenge the right of eleven people to stand as candidates for ATSIC. He claimed they were not Aborigines. The judge was plainly unhappy at having to examine lines of descent; he was prepared to give the benefit of the doubt to people who had a strong family tradition that there was an Aboriginal ancestor. He excluded only two of the eleven, saying that today identity is much more social than genetic. In effect he relaxed an already loose definition. This might not matter too much when the issue is standing for ATSIC, but if under a treaty a class of people with special legal rights was being defined, this looseness would be unacceptable.

Cassandra Pybus, who gave evidence in this case, is sure that some people accepted by the judge have no Aboriginal ancestor. All their ancestors were settlers. She notes the sad irony of this outcome. The descendants of those who shot the Aborigines and took their land are now receiving benefits earmarked for Aborigines.

Many people do not recognise how well integrated Aborigines are. When they think of Aborigines, they think of tribal people in the outback; they don't think of suburbanites who have been suburbanites for three generations. Consider this household. The husband is Aboriginal of mixed descent; one of his four grandparents was Aboriginal. His wife is of English, Scots, Irish and Italian descent. Their oldest daughter in her late teens becomes interested in her Aboriginal heritage. Her siblings show no interest. She declares that she is Aboriginal and seeks out other Aborigines. There can be no objection to this; it is a free country. But is it seriously proposed that by treaty she should officially be declared indigenous, that she acquire special rights, and that she be given compensation for the loss of her ancestral land, language and culture? The notion is absurd.

A treaty has been criticised as divisive. It certainly would be, and in a more profound sense than is commonly realised. The division and the bitterness would begin with the act of defining who the Aborigines are. It would give members of the same family a different status. Remember, in a majority of Aboriginal households the couples are mixed.

The marrying and partnering of people of all sorts across all boundaries is the great unifying force in Australia. The United States never saw a melting pot that melted so rapidly. It will produce before too long a new people who will have darker skins, much better suited to this place and our sun.

In fifty years there may still be buskers in Martin Place and they may play didgeridoos, but the observer will no longer be able to label them Anglo-Celt or Vietnamese; they will have no other name than Australian. I am sorry I will not live to see that day, for the Australians are going to be a beautiful people.

ENDNOTES

1. James Jupp (ed.), *Encyclopedia of the Australian People*, Angus and Robertson, Sydney, 1988, pp. 127-8, 463, 528, 898; F.L. Jones, *Ancestry Groups in Australia: A Descriptive Overview*, AGPS, Canberra, 1991, p. 34.
2. Quoted in Jupp, ibid., pp. 127-8. Emphasis added.
3. Nadia Wheatley, *Five Times Dizzy*, Hodder Children's Books, Sydney, 1997.
4. Yasmine Gooneratne, *A Change of Skies*, Picador Australia, Sydney, 1981.

MARY KALANTZIS

Recognising diversity

HISTORY BY NUMBERS

The fetish we have for numbers has just landed us in 2001. And this number tells us it's time to remember an Australian event of a century ago—the Federation of the Australian colonies. For a few years in the last decade of the twentieth century, it seemed we might have been able to make something of the numerology. We thought we might be able to make the number 2001 iconic of another moment of historical transition. But, for reasons that don't bear repeating, the push to redefine Australia as a republic came unstuck before the anointed year.

Having a moment for national reflection reduced to a mere number is, I suppose, appropriate to our times, metaphysically speaking, as everything in our cultural world is progressively reduced to an invisible base code in which zeros and ones are expanded into multiples of ten before they become words, sounds and images. Despite the rapidity with which we are being propelled into the future by the forces of the digital age, paradoxically we seem to have stopped thinking much about the cultural qualities of the present compared with those of the past, let alone about how we might achieve more sociable futures.

The centenary of Federation was a moment that promised us the opportuntiy to reimagine ourselves and take pride in our achievements. But, by and large, we have done little more than attempt to retouch the image of Federation, to retell the story within its original terms of reference. The newspaper stories have been half-hearted. And we have tended to doze off in front of our TV screens when the Federation story comes on, only to be woken by cricket scandals, horror stories from our very own concentration camps and the tale of the tennis star who defected from an Australia in which she and her family could no longer feel at home to a Yugoslavia in which, it seems, they can.

What a lost opportunity. For by remembering in this purely celebratory but inevitably half-hearted way, we have really been forgetting. Deliberately forgetting.

We are forgetting that the primary motivation for Federation, the only issue on which Australia really wanted to maintain an independent line from London, was race. Federation set in place three distinctively local initiatives: White Australia, protection of the industry and trade of White Men and a regime of racial separation for Aborigines. The first two provided the new Commonwealth with some of its finest and most impassioned public rhetoric. The last was a new way of still not having to speak about historical processes that, had one chosen to talk, could have justifiably been called invasion and genocide.

Had it been possible in this moment to remember truly, we would have been able to take enormous pride not only in what is the same about Australia in 2001 as in 1901, but in how much we have changed, and we would have been able to take heart also in the promise inherent in this self-tranformation, the promise of what we could still be. This would have been indeed an interesting story.

Sad to say, I don't think we're good at knowing our history in Australia.

Take one emblematic site in another country with a troubled history—Germany. And whether today's Germany is a country that should be more troubled or less by its history than today's Australia is an entirely irrelevant question. The site I want to mention is the new Federal Foreign Office, opened in Berlin a year ago. This building is modern Germany's point of contact with the world, a Germany that is today the economic and political linchpin, as well as the future geographical centre of a federated Europe. It also houses the new office of the highest-ranking Green politician in the world, Foreign Minister Joschka Fischer. But it is a building with a terrible and still palpable history. Constructed as the Nazi Reichsbank, the design was personally chosen by Hitler in 1933. The modernist Mies van der Rohe had submitted an entry to the design competition, but the one chosen instead epitomised the emerging Nazi aesthetics.

And then the building lived up to its aesthetics. Not only was this where financing of the Nazi war machine was planned and executed, but reportedly where the gold teeth of Nazi victims were melted down. Then, after the war, it was rebuilt as the offices of the Central Committee of the East German Communist Party. In the 1959 reconstruction another heavy aesthetic layer was added, the aesthetics of the Stalinist Third International. When the decision was made in 1999 to make this building the new Foreign Office, a furious public debate erupted. The debate was not about whether either of the meanings of the two former layers of history should in any sense be restored, but about how to start history afresh. Were the ghosts in this place so repugnant that it should be demolished?

No, it was decided that the future be made through an act of historical transformation of the old structure, yet an act that is at the same time one of always-having-to-remember. The solution was to leave both the two former layers of historical meaning partially intact and to add a third layer of meaning to the building—and, the ultimate act of aesthetic defiance, the Mies van der Rohe furniture. The hope for the future is in the consciousness of this layering, in the deliberate juxtaposition of motifs from 1933, 1959, and 1999, in remembering the past and deliberately contrasting the past with the present.

This is not the stuff of guilt or of younger generations having to take personal responsibililty for the sins of older generations. Rather, it is an act of moral self-definition, and the insistence that always history should be remembered—and this is the only guarantee that the future will be better.

But what of our capacity to remember?

PAST AS PROLOGUE

In fact, there are two Australian federation stories. In the first, our history is entirely different from Germany's. In the second, we have been similarly modern people.

Federation story No 1 runs like this. The first nation to be founded at the ballot box, Australia is arguably one of the oldest and most stable of liberal democracies. The

Federation compact was built on the politics of peaceful compromise rather than bloody revolution. Coming at the end of a decade of virulent class struggle, Federation represents the moment of class accommodation. It was the moment in which the world's first government of the working class was elected—and this with the consent, albeit begrudging and temporary, of the ruling class. It was a moment in which unions were institutionalised as part of the fabric of society and class conflict was regulated through legal processes of industrial arbitration. It was the moment of social welfare, the creation of a basic living wage, the eight-hour day and regulated working conditions. The result was standards of living not rivalled anywhere else in the world, with less disparity in wealth between classes than any other place. This is how Australia averted the communisms and the fascisms that plagued other parts of the world—Germany, for instance.

Australia has also, in this story, been a peaceful place. No wars have been fought on Australian shores. We have fought in other people's wars, to be sure, but provoked none. So, too, we have become a place where our history is not characteristic of our geography. We have been a shining light of Anglo-European progress and civilisation in a region of gross underdevelopment at worst and horribly uneven development at best, a region governed mostly by authoritarian and often corrupt regimes.

This is the story of the Australian nation on its own terms. By world historical standards it's not a bad story, and it's true.

By telling this story in this year of remembering, we have chosen to ennoble the founding fathers—and the leading roles they played in the processes of drafting the

Constitution, voting for its adoption, and the inauguration of the Commonwealth of Australia. We have found these men to be decent, if uninspiring, fellows.

But there's another Federation story. Only around 25.5 per cent of the eligible adult population bothered to vote in the referendum that created the Commonwealth. The Constitution document, drafted in Australia and subsequently enacted in the Westminster parliament, is purely procedural, dividing powers between the Commonwealth and the states. It is not even a document that could be called democratic in its fundamental character. There was no mention of universal franchise (because there wasn't such a franchise; most women couldn't vote until the Franchise Act of 1902, an Act that at the same time explicitly barred Aborigines from voting). There was no mention of voting as a right (because these rights could be determined in a racially discriminatory way, and were). There was no mention of the rule of law. There was no mention of citizens and their rights (because Australians were still subjects of the Imperial monarch). There was no mention of freedom of speech or association. And the pinnacle of the constitutional system was an all-powerful unelected head of state whose Australian representative could 'at his pleasure' appoint an executive council to rule.

This was hardly a moment that could be called the making of a 'nation' in the sense of an independent power whose sovereignty rested in the people. Australia was unequivocally a part of the British Empire and its people were subjects, not citizens. 'We are not disposed to give any countenance to the novel doctrine that there is an Australian nationality as distinguished from a British nationality', the High Court said in 1906.[1] In fact, Federation was not even an act of independence on the part of Australians. Federation was what the imperial government had wanted for Australia as early as 1846, a suggestion for local and more consistent self-government in the interest of Empire and a suggestion that the colonists had, from London's point of view, been painfully slow to take up.

The one point of difference with the imperial government was on the question of race. This was the only thing distinctively Australian about Federation, and if there was an Australian nationalism, albeit a relatively weak nationalism, this was its essence. Within the idea of race were the issues of immigration, trade and Aborigines.

Immigration had been, in a practical sense, almost unrestricted until the closing decades of the nineteenth century. This was not just a matter of imperial pragmatics, although it was that—the pragmatics of open borders and open labour markets in the era of *laissez-faire* capitalism and a pragmatics in which Pacific Island labour was used in the sugar plantations of the tropics and near-tropics, Afghans to drive the camel trains across desert interiors, Chinese to work over the goldfields and set up market gardens, Malays and Japanese to dive for pearls. It was also a matter of imperial principle. At the Intercolonial Conference of 1897 Mr Chamberlain, Britain's Secretary of State for the Colonies, reminded the Australians who at the time had resolved to adopt the 'dictation test' to restrict coloured immigration, of their greater imperial responsibilities: 'We ask you also to bear in mind the traditions of Empire, which make no distinction in favour of or against race or colour'.[2]

However, distinctions in favour and against race the Australians nevertheless were to make, and make in no uncertain terms. Two of the first major pieces of legislation in the Commonwealth parliament were to be the Immigration Restriction Act banning coloured immigration, and the Pacific Island Labourers' Act to repatriate the South Sea Islanders working in the Queensland sugar plantations.

Imperial principle was replaced by distinctively Australian principle, described by our first prime minister, Edmund Barton, in one of his finer rhetorical moments thus:

The doctrine of the equality of man was never intended to apply to the equality of the Englishman and the Chinaman. There is a deep-set difference, and we see no prospect and no promise of its ever being effaced. Nothing in this world can put these two races upon an equality. Nothing we can do by cultivation, by refinement, or by anything else will make some races equal to others.[3]

The leader of the party of the working class, J.C. Watson, agreed. And on the primary objective of Federation, Alfred Deakin, the first attorney-general, was clear, that, 'we should be one people, and remain one people, without admixture of other races'.[4]

Another Australian difference with the imperial government was on the issue of trade. In the mid nineteenth century, at the height of British colonial rule, Australia was a place of *laissez-faire* economics and free trade. Federation marked a sharp turn away from these imperial principles, a turn founded on the idea that the interests of the national economy were antithetical to the interests of international economy in which inferior and lowly paid races might unfairly compete against Australians, whose industry was based on high wages.

So the Australians erected high tariff walls. After the class conflicts of the 1890s it was agreed that the state should interfere in the market for the mutual benefit of both classes. Race was the linchpin of the compromise between classes, the agreement to civilise capitalism. The material benefits of industrial arbitration could only be afforded with the protection of high tariff barriers. It was only possible to replace the South Sea Island labourers on the sugar canefields of north-eastern Australia with better-paid white labour if there was a tariff on sugar imports and a bounty on sugar production.

Insofar as Federation was a moment of nation-making and insofar as those making it were becoming something other than subjects of empire, it was around a package of compromises to regulate the market, and this for the benefit of a nation personified as 'Australians'. Tariffs protected not the rights of man but the rights of 'Australians' against the unfair competion of other races.

The other main difference between Australians and the imperial government was over Aborigines. In the relative silence that continued to veil the processes of invasion and genocide, Federation marked a new way of not speaking about the fate of formerly sovereign indigenous nations. Or, at least, barely speaking about them, or speaking about them only in order to state how they would not be spoken about. Aboriginal people were mentioned only twice in the new Constitution—and both times to legislate their absence (in Section 51 (xxvi), and Section 127). The first prohibited the Commonwealth from making 'special laws' for the Aboriginal 'race' and the second prohibited their being counted 'in reckoning the numbers of the people of the Commonwealth'.

This framework for not speaking about Aborigines was quite new and locally devised. At the height of British colonial rule a serious effort had been made, if not always successfully, to ensure that Aborigines enjoyed certain rights, at the very least those of people who had become British subjects by virtue of conquest. They could not be murdered indiscriminately; their lands could not be taken without compensatory measures; their lives could not be disrupted without assuming some kind of duty of care. This tradition began with Governor Phillip's instructions to negotiate with the inhabitants of the continent when he arrived in 1788. It was an approach that continued through to Colonial Secretary Earl Grey's instructions in the late 1840s that the colonies were to establish large-scale reservations for Aborigines so they could continue to provide for themselves. Grey also insisted that the pastoral leases that recognised the expanding squatter settlement were for pasturage only and that Aboriginal people had 'mutual' property rights. The reality, however, was an unspoken war on the part of the frontiersmen who couldn't be further away from London, geographically speaking, as well in their own intentions and actions. The truths of invasion and the destruction of indigenous nations during the colonial period were the silent and mostly illegal *modus operandi* of the so-called 'settlers'.

This ineffectual imperial framework of rights was abandoned in the era of Federation. A new way of not having to speak about Aborigines, called without irony 'Aboriginal protection', emerged around the time of Federation and was to last halfway into the twentieth century. This evolved into a system that institutionalised Aboriginal people on reserves, a system so authoritarian as to amount in many cases almost to incarceration. Aborigines were put into the same category as prisoners and lunatics in a society that was, at the time, busily setting up 'modern' institutions to remove every manner of social evil and place such evils out of sight and therefore out of mind. At the same time 'mixed race' children were removed from the reserves and from their families. It was thought that interbreeding with whites would at least give them a chance. For the remaining Aborigines, however, it was a matter of 'smoothing the pillow of a dying race', to quote a phrase in common use at the time. As an inferior race and a primitive culture, modern rationality held they were destined to disappear. Racial segregation, removal of citizenship rights—these were the new nation's new solutions to the burden of a history that had begun with invasion and ended in genocide.

TRUE TO OURSELVES

When we dare to tell this second and more difficult story of Federation, it's a modern story that, in its fundamental shape, is not dissimilar to Germany's. The big-picture ideas are no different from those of the German 1930s and 1940s: of the necessity to create 'one people . . . without admixture of races' (to use Deakin's words again); of unbridgeable racial inferiority, of races destined to die out and of the eugenics of progress. Nor were the technologies of race management so dissimilar: the enforced separation in concentration camps, the petty regulation of freedoms of movement and association. Nor, too, were the effects so different—in the Australian case, a genocide in which

90 per cent of the Aboriginal population died over the period of a century, and the wholesale destruction of peoples with distinctive languages and ways of life.

In the first story of Federation, 1901 represents a high point in Australian history. In the second story, it is probably the lowest. Told on its own, Story No 1 is a way of using the process of remembering in order to forget, of selective memory as a way of forgetting through omission. Story No 2 is of course a much harder one to tell, being bound up with the problem of remembering things you don't want to remember, of recalling things that are painful to remember. The problem, of course, is that there are not really two stories. The logic of Federation in the second version of events was inseparable from the logic of the first.

To be true to ourselves, we must struggle to tell both stories as one. This is not for the sake of wallowing in angst, or using the sins of past generations to visit the consciences of present generations. This is no black armband view of history, no uncovering of truths that require us forever to mourn. If race was the primary motivating force for Federation, it is hardly worth asking whether the Australian solution was right for then. The only point is that it is wrong for now, an utterly unconscionable means to achieve any contemporary or future end. When it comes to the past, guilt is of no use. We just need recognition and perhaps even retrospective forgiveness for those who were creatures of their time and who did incidental, collateral harm rather than premeditated harm.

The good thing about the Federation story, the whole story in which version No 1 and version No 2 of historical events are inseparable, is not just the continuities of the first version, but the transformations of the second. This is how even the second verison of the story can become a source of pride.

Immigration Over the second half of the twentieth century, we have had the largest immigration program of any country in the world relative to existing population, bar the peculiar case of Israel. This led to the enactment of the Australian Nationality and Citizenship Act in 1948. The population has grown from seven to nineteen million, half because of immigration. Forty-one per cent of the Australian population has one parent born overseas. It has also been the most diverse program of any country in the world. The society that has been created can only be described as multicultural, a term now used universally but that slipped into the lexicon in Australia before any other place in the world, bar Canada, where it meant something less than its Australian and now contemporary international meanings. The multicultural idea came to be used as a policy prescription from the mid 1970s, as a series of cultural rights and as a framework through which government would relate to civil society. This development coincided with the first large-scale influx of non-white immigrants since the nineteenth century, and the definitive demise of the practice of White Australia.

Trade We have progressively shifted our view of the world, from being an alien place populated by hostile outsiders to a place of exchange and opportunity. As a percentage of national product, Australia is one of the most export-oriented countries on earth. The basis for this exchange has also changed. Whereas the Federation compact quarantined Australia in order to protect the living standards of white men, we now set out to exchange goods or services on the market because we are particularly good at making or providing them. And we have progressively shifted our exports away from commodities and raw materials towards value-added products and high-contact quintessentially intercultural industries such as education and tourism. You are what you do, and the frame of reference within which you do it changes your sensibilities. From being a parochial country that fears the outside world we have become a cosmopolitan nation that reaches out and engages with the world.

Indigenous peoples The 1967 referendum removed the sections of the Constitution that excluded Aborigines from the Commonwealth. The 1992 Mabo decision recognised residual rights to Crown lands. The 1996 Wik decision recognised overlapping rights of Aboriginal people in the pastoral leases that cover 40 per cent of the continent. The *Bringing them Home* report of 1997 documented and recognised the iniquities of removing so-called mixed race children from their Aboriginal parents and the racial theories upon which this practice was based. In 2000, the reconciliation movement brought out the largest crowds to support any social or political cause in Australian history, in a statement of support for an accommodation between indigenous and settler societies. And now there's serious discussion of the possibility of a treaty that recognises the sovereign rights of Aboriginal and Torres Strait Islander peoples. Despite all the progress we have made, there can be little doubt that the bonds of our civil society have become frayed in recent years—the disengagement of government from the reconciliation process; the retreat from multiculturalism; the paranoia about immigration and refugees; the anxiety about our neighbours and globalisation.

We need urgently to renew our civic soul, to engage seriously and honestly with indigenous issues, to appreciate how immigration contributes to our economy and remaking of our local identity, to define who we are in Asia, facilitate our global economic interests and to create a modern democratic constitution that truly represents what we have become and still can be.

On the question of our Constitution there is an enormous amount to be done, a much larger question than deleting from the text mention of a completely ineffectual head of state. We have a *de facto* democracy but not a *de jure* democracy, a country that functions like a democracy but without a democratic constitution. The Australian Constitution is a profoundly flawed and inadequate document that does little service to any of the principles, rights and responsibilities of democracy. In fact, we have a constitution that in places includes shameful legacies and continues vividly to express the spirit of the time of its drafting. Section 25, which still makes provisions as to races 'disqualified from voting', is a case in point.

Nation without ethnos

At root, the men of 1901 were facing the same issue we face in 2001, the issue of identity and the dynamics of belonging. In one respect, our response to this issue today is—and must be—diametrically opposed to theirs. This opposition turns on one word: diversity.

Our founders responded to diversity in the process of forging Australian identity and creating a sense of belonging to the new nation with the formula: one people, one culture, one nation. It drew a neat boundary defining who could belong, and on what terms. But how must we respond today in an area of ever more intensely localised identity politics and globalised structures that promote rapidly increasing inter-cultural contact?

Answers to this conundrum have already been created, tested and reworked in Australia, more usefully in the second half of the twentieth century than in the first. In our workplaces we have developed a kind of productive diversity in which differences are the wellspring of energy and creativity and diversity is used as a resource to reach into local niche and dispersed local markets. In our civic lives we have created the idea of multiculturalism, not just as a description of the brightly coloured wallpaper that is our contemporary cultural reality—the stuff of festivals and street parades—but also as a series of local agreements, founded on a new social contract, to live together in our difference. And in our personal lives, we have become new people, more outward-looking, more cosmopolitan, more tolerant.

A lot is bundled into this idea of diversity. It's not just based in differences in ethnic origins or the differences between indigenous and settler experiences. It's also captured in the spirit of the Gay and Lesbian Mardi Gras, the biggest event in the Australian calendar as well as the biggest event of its kind in the world. And, more broadly, the way we live in and with our diversity is the sign of a deep epistemological and moral shift, a shift in the way we understand our identities and the ways in which we make the accommodations that add up to sociability. We have, in short, managed in fits and starts to build a new ethics, as well as a new pragmatics, of cohabitation.

This trajectory represents a kind of historical journey, and by following the direction of that journey we can perhaps divine our country's destiny. We have been on the way to creating a state without *ethnos* and a community without nation. We have been developing a post-nationalist civics after a world century racked by selective inclusions and often vicious exclusions on the basis of *ethnos*, or race. This destiny, both as an ideal and as a pragmatic reading of the flow of our history, I would call a state of 'civic pluralism'.

Negotiating diversity is now the only way to produce social cohesion. Pluralistic citizenship is the most effective way of holding things together, and an outward-looking, internationalist approach to the world is now the only way to maintain the national interest. This requires a paradoxical new universal in which negotiating differences becomes the national essence. The state needs to assume a dual task: to develop community whilst securing diversity and to create pathways for all whilst respecting differences. This will not happen automatically; indeed, it may not happen at all. But it is something that needs to be imagined as a possibility, an ideal for which we can strive.

We have not yet been sufficiently clear-sighted to write down what it is we have achieved, not in a constitutional sense and not even in our contemporary retellings of the Federation story. Hope lies in the everyday, in the inchoate flows of civil society, in organic processes of self-transformation that often elude our attention.

We're a lucky country, as Donald Horne has famously (and ironically) told us, prosperous and comfortable despite our leaders. And, from this truth will surely emerge a modern democratic constitution, a flag that includes all of us, affinity with our region, inclusive symbols of belonging and a treaty with the sovereign nations displaced without negotiation by the British Empire and its successor, the Commonwealth of Australia.

In the first week of the new Australian century I attended a wedding in Townsville. The marriage was between a young woman of Irish Catholic background and a young Aboriginal man. Her parents are academics and they had brought up their children in the Kimberley and the USA before moving to Townsville—Irish people of the world and Australians through and through. His family was from Palm Island, a tropical paradise and, not so long ago, a hellish concentration camp. He had played rugby league for the North Queensland Cowboys then become a plumber. Both were now students at the university, the young woman studying business and the young man medicine. These achievements were barely mentioned in the many speeches. The cultural heritages were interwoven: clapsticks and emu dancing; larrikin exuberance and Irish irreverence; all mixed with lace and flowers and bridesmaids in pale blue.

Marriage vows, white dresses, tiered wedding cakes. And other Australian touches, like the *bombonières*—those fancy little parcels of sugared almonds traditionally distributed at Greek and Italian weddings as a symbol of fertility. They are not Greek or Italian any longer, but near-universal in north Queensland, where the migrants in the sugar industry have turned something exotic and strange into something ordinary and touching. Something for everybody.

This is Australia, 100 years after Federation.

ENDNOTES

1. *Attorney-General (Commonwealth) v. Ah Sheung* (1966) 4CLR 949, 961.
2. Quoted in Myra Willard, *History of the White Australia Policy*, Melbourne University Press, Melbourne, 1923, p. 112.
3. Commonwealth Parliamentary Debates, 26 September 1901, p. 5233.
4. Quoted in Willard, *op. cit.*, p. 110.

8

LYDIA MILLER

Recognition of the past . . . Reconciliation in the future . . . Restitution now

I would like to give my respect to and honour the ancestors of the Eora, the Cadigal, the Gadigal and the Dharruk, on whose lands I speak.

Indigenous peoples have occupied their lands since time immemorial, so far back into the beginnings of humanity that it is seemingly irrelevant whether it is 60,000 years or 100,000 years or a million years. The ancestors of peoples who owned and occupied these lands around Sydney are not usurped by our presence, but are forever an integral part of our history and our future. Ironically, Customs House, the venue for this lecture, is also where the first flag of the colony was placed. What an auspicious site of significance, as we look to the past to interpret our future.

As Oodgeroo Noonuccal of the lands of Minjerriba wrote so eloquently, 'Let no-one say the past is dead, the past is all about us and within . . .'. I would like to quote a poem of hers that resonates with the intention of these Barton Lectures.

Understand, old one,
I mean no desecration
Staring here with the learned ones
At your opened grave.
Now after hundreds of years gone
The men of science coming with spade and knowledge
Peer and probe, handle the yellow bones,
To them specimens, to me
More. Deeply moved am I.

Understand, old one,
I mean no lack of reverence.
It is with love
I think of you so long ago laid here
With tears and wailing.
Strongly I feel your presence very near
Haunting the old spot, watching
As we disturb your bones. Poor ghost,
I know, I know you will understand.

What if you came back now
To our new world, the city roaring

There on the old peaceful camping place
Of your red fires along the quiet water,
How would you wonder
At towering stone gunyas high in air
Immense, incredible;
Planes in the sky over, swarms of cars
like things frantic in flight.
What if you came at night upon these miles
Of clustered neon lights of all colours
Like Christian newly come to his Heaven or Hell
And your own people gone?
Old one of so long ago,
So many generations lie between us
But cannot estrange. Your duty to your race
Was with the simple past, mine
Lies in the present and the coming days.[1]

Recognition of the past calls for recognition of the people who have shaped what we are today, as well as recognising that we today will shape the future for those who follow us. What we do in the present will determine the nature of the society we leave as our legacy to future generations, but more than this, it is by our actions and deeds that the future will judge us. The future we hold in our mind's eye. We dare to imagine a world of infinite possibilities in which hope springs eternal, where experience makes us wiser and where we suspend our disbelief to believe in the moment of 'what if'. If recognition of the past equates with our wisdom, and reconciliation is our hope for a shared future, then surely restitution is the journey toward our destination as a community and a nation.

Australia celebrates one hundred years of Federation.

However, the framing of a constitution does not necessarily equate either with a nation's maturity or with wisdom about how the state may honour its contract with the people. Instead, Australia's early years of political organisation demonstrate not any real embodiment of democracy and political philosophy, but that political ideology and its counterpart, political opportunism, have ruled as Australia's political *raison d'être*. Australia's unique geographical position and relative isolation from Europe have given birth to a society whose members have unique insights into how democracy is imagined and manifested. If we are capable of imagining that we are the sum total of our atomic parts and we believe that Australia has reached political maturity and wisdom, recognition of the rights of those citizens disempowered by the state needs to be addressed as a matter of political principle: otherwise, why should the state receive endorsement from those it so actively disempowers? Restitution is the state's responsibility to fulfil its charter to its citizens from whom it derives its very power. To deny or refute the fact that restitution is a priority is to perpetuate the myth of Australia's democracy while consolidating the rise of an authoritarian state.

The writing of Australia's Constitution took ten years, from 1891 to 1901. During that time the self-proclaimed ruling elites and the squattocracy managed to ensure that their power base was firmly entrenched, their economic interests consolidated and their domination over Aborigines, women and others was determined. It is ironic, then, that in a parallel ten-year period from 1991 to 2001 the Council for Aboriginal Reconciliation failed to garner the necessary endorsement from the same ruling elites to ensure a document for reconciliation that would invest the moral and ethical attributes of nationhood.

Perhaps the imperative of nationhood and the resolution of Australia's relationship with its indigenous people were not really part of the intention of the Federation of the Commonwealth. And thus, Australian democracy is still an oxymoron. While the superficial rhetoric is espoused, including majority rule and representative democracy, the continuing exclusion from the political process of Aborigines, Torres Strait Islanders and other disempowered groups reveals how democracy is considered in the most narrow and insular of interpretations in Australia. This is very different from the classical notion that the state derives its power from the people or the polity, and that the individual and the group rely on it as an agent to uphold and protect their rights and freedoms. The social contract is more than an adminstrative entity ensuring the functionality of its components; it is about notions of rights and freedoms, about the contract of entrusted autonomy.

If those who constitute the state are not prepared to act in a manner that enfranchises the polity, why should Aborigines as a polity entrust their autonomy to such a dangerous institution? One that conducts itself according to the dictates of political opportunism and expediency, actively seeking to disenfranchise the rights, freedoms, and accordingly, the very existence of Indigenous people, has no validity. If the state can manifest a democratic political philosophy ensuring the integrity of each of its members while refuting its ideological premise of opportunism, it is paramount that it seeks restitution as a political principle.

At the beginning of the twenty-first century, Australia is a unique and diverse nation affording a home to some eighteen million people. Aboriginal and Torres Strait Islanders constitute some 1.8 per cent of the population. Yet we have the profile of Fourth World peoples. Our civil, political, economic, social and cultural record is a source of shame for such an affluent nation-state. 'Compared with other Australians, Indigenous people experience poorer health, limited employment opportunities, educational disadvantage and greater imprisonment.'[2] While we may wax lyrical about Australia as a nation, imbuing ourselves with a collective spirit about what it is to be 'Australian', it is ultimately Australia's conduct as a nation-state that will determine whether or not we have reached political and civic maturity and wisdom.

We are an imagined nation; we identify as Australians through what exists in our imaginations. We imagine that we are who we are as a people because we promulgate symbols, iconography, images and words that reinforce our sense of belonging, our sense of community and our sense of identity. That we choose to reaffirm our sense of identity in the public arena through participation with the wider community indicates some commonly held notions of what it is to be Australian today. What those abstract notions are, however, exist in the realm of our imaginations—we continually negotiate with each other to determine and define them. Yet we yearn for an imagined nation where we can transcend our interminable differences in our social structures, our beliefs, our prejudices, and allow ourselves a moment of wonder at the richness of the society we have through the contribution of the many. We ask ourselves 'what if . . .' and fumble for an expression of what we may become as a nation.

The centenary of Federation was perceived as a

symbolic occasion for addressing Australia's uneasy relationship with its Indigenous people. In 1994 the Centenary of Federation Advisory Committee published its report, *2001, A Report from Australia* emphasising the opportunity to redefine Australia's nationhood and highlighting that one of the most important issues was reconciliation. 'It is imperative that there be an assessment of the progress made on reconciliation. Without meaningful progress in the reconciliation process there will be no truly national celebration.'

What are we celebrating, then, in the centenary of Federation in 2001?

We can celebrate the changing culture of Australia where the awareness of Indigenous people has increased. The rise of indigenous art and culture has highlighted the nature of Indigenous cultural paradigms. Stories, songs, dances and paintings demonstrate the interconnectedness of Indigenous art, culture, heritage, relationships to the land and the sea, and customary law where political, economic and social issues are interwoven. Today, it is not surprising to have a 'welcome to country', Indigenous dancers opening events, large international touring exhibitions or indigenous theatrical works, rock concerts and Indigenous literature being studied in schools and universities. It is through art and culture that the identity and diversity of Indigenous people is asserted, and where non-Indigenous Australians begin their journey of understanding the world inhabited by Indigenous people, as told by Indigenous people.

The Sydney 2000 Olympics, especially the opening ceremony, intrigued all Australians. It was such a statement of immense symbolic images, it made us stare transfixed and disbelieving that this is the sum total of who and what we are. We were amazed by the pageantry and beauty of the Australia we now live in. Some sections resonated so deeply with knowing that we were overwhelmed, as if intoxicated with the scent of our essence as a nation. What a magnificent, complex, rich and mesmerising essence—knowing we were more than inflatable kangaroos on bikes. We were entranced by the many elements of who we are—our relationship to the sea, the ancient culture of Aboriginal people and Torres Strait Islanders, the beauty of our land, the early years of the colony, the Tin Symphony, the arrival of migrants, and finally the symbols that the working class and their energy had built this country we call home.[3]

For many Australians, the Olympics were a watershed. Endless media commentaries told us we had reached maturity as a nation. We watched as athletes in all fields strove to do their personal best and when Cathy Freeman ran, Australia stood still for forty-nine seconds. The closing ceremony was all the more telling for its symbolism, too; when Midnight Oil revealed the word 'sorry' written on their clothing we cheered in support; the fact that they had done so without the prior awareness of those in authority resonated widely. Christine Anu and Yothu Yindi articulated our love for our land and our most pressing issue: a treaty. We laughed when larger-than-life symbols of modern Australia threaded together seemingly disparate elements of who we are, from kewpie dolls to Mambo. The Olympics saw many Australians in theatres and boardrooms, in offices and on the streets, transfixed as day after day something was unveiled about their Australia, our Australia. Yet we are all these things and more.

We are capable of recognising that there is a great deal of unresolved business in the relationship between Indigenous and non-Indigenous Australia. The reconciliation walk across the Sydney Harbour Bridge symbolised one of the most fundamental issues we face as Australians. Half a million people crossed the bridge; people came from all walks of life to show that they were a visible symbol for reconciliation. Under clear blue sky emblazoned with the word 'sorry', they joined hands with fellow Australians and breathed life into the nation; an echo of the 'Sea of Hands' exhibition that toured the length and breadth of Australia. That exhibition was a potent symbol of the desire of many Australians for reconciliation, seemingly anonymous by their absence, yet very much present in the landscape of Australia's deliberations on reconciliation. Across Australia many people signed the 'sorry' books to articulate what the state was incapable of saying. That Australians had engaged for some ten years in the countless workshops held throughout the country to consider how we might move forward in this country to calling ourselves a united Australia is testimony to the fact that we know we have serious work to do before we are ever truly comfortable about who and what we are.

We examined our prejudices, stereotypes and history to formalise our disparate and common goals into a document to be presented to the government as a symbol of the deliberations of its citizens, articulating the formal position of the people. That document began with a future hope envisioning 'a united Australia which respects this land of ours, values the Aboriginal and Torres Strait Islander heritage and provides justice and equity for all'. Reconciliation has stirred a nation's conscience. It is a symbol that we want to achieve as a reality for our community and our nation. That this document now lies in some government office gathering dust is an insult to the people. People put government into power and it follows that they can remove governments from power. To date, the people have instructed the government that this issue is a substantive principle and a central issue for the nation.

If reconciliation is perceived as attainable in the future we need to ask ourselves: how long and which aspect of reconciliation? It is not enough to believe that the formal responses can wait and languish, subject to political opportunism. The social justice imperative of reconciliation requires action now, as it did in 2000. It requires the formal acceptance of the civil, political, economic, social and cultural changes necessary to ensure that a united Australia reflects our respect for our land and seas, our valuing of the heritage of Aboriginal people and Torres Strait Islanders and that we are a just and equitable nation-state. If we take care of all of these aspects of the reconciliation process, the future will be the society we have created. The future belongs to our children; it is they who will be the beneficiaries of our moral and ethical legacy. Reconciliation will be our political high water mark as a nation.

Let the symbols of the future resonate with truth and substance. Let us not let them become a cynical, dismissive exercise of bread and circuses for the nation. We are a decent people and we are not fools. When the rest of the world is tearing itself apart through cultural and racial power plays, let us have the courage to be the sum total of our many parts, to demand that we be united through our diversity.

For reconciliation, the focus needs to be an institutional, structural collaborative, co-operative reform. It is about a fundamental shift from welfare to basic rights, from dependence to autonomy, from government assistance to power. Central to this is Indigenous self-determination. It is not about mimicking non-Indigenous determinations of what is good for us; it is about the right to determine our future as a fundamental premise of asserting our authority and autonomy as Indigenous peoples.

Throughout Australian history, every step towards the recognition of our rights to live and exist within our homelands has been fought for and fought hard. Every single day. From the right to be served in a shop or to have running water or a job to the right to have title to our lands recognised, our culture recognised, our status as Indigenous people recognised, recognition that we are citizens of the nation-state called Australia, we are focused on achieving not only collective rights as Indigenous people as recognised under international law, but also citizen rights as expounded under domestic law.

If the Constitution took a mere ten years for realisation, why has not a document for reconciliation been achieved in ten years?

At the beginning of 1891, when Edmund Barton and others began the push for a constitution, Indigenous people had already lived through their first centenary of struggle for recognition in their own lands under a foreign military regime. What that centenary represented then is perhaps no different from what the centenary of Federation represents today—bread and circuses under an authoritarian regime. As it was then, so it is now. There is no reserved seat at the table of power for indigenous people, for those seats are reserved—as they have always been reserved throughout Australian history—for those who derive their power from ensuring the continuation of inequitable relationships between Indigenous and non-Indigenous peoples. Inequity has as its basis the war between Indigenous and non-Indigenous people where land and culture were, and still are, the central issues.

These fundamental grievances will not vanish without restitution. Recognition of the past highlights the fact that there were no treaties, no formal settlements, no compacts. Aboriginal people and Torres Strait Islanders did not cede sovereignty to their lands, and it is that issue that will remain a continuing source of dispute. In looking to the past for corroboration I would ask, where are the Eora and the Cadigal?; where are those peoples who watched the ships come in so long ago, and who are conspicuous by their absence in these times? Why do the Dharug, the Wiradjuri, the Gamilaroi, the Pitjantjatjara, the Kooma, the Wik, the Wandji, the Gugu Yalandji, the Bundjalung, the Larrakia, the Noonuccal, the Indinji, the Walpiri, the Pintupi continually assert their identity and their culture?

In 1900, with the promulgation of the Constitution and the consolidation of the economic and land interests of the ruling elites and the squattocracy—who obtained their status by means of the subjugation of Indigenous peoples—opportunism was the political *raison d'être* and democracy was a politically correct term derived from those bastions of English privilege and American self-interest. In 1901 Aborigines were living on missions and reserves akin to concentration camps, where their movements were controlled by the state, and the state and its control over Indigenous people has been a continual motif in the relationship with Indigenous people. Essentially these relations have been about the state maintaining its controlling interests, and in this lies the foundation of Indigenous people seeking self-determination. Indigenous people controlling their interests is a fundamental tenet of restitution. Whether the state chooses to endorse that tenet or maintain its opportunistic interests is at the heart of Australia's current debate on reconciliation.

During this period the state actively legislated for the establishment of reserves and missions throughout Australia. In the 1930s the policy of assimilation was touted by the state. Indigenous peoples were to be assimilated, irrespective of their wishes. The emphasis was on those who were considered 'detribalised'. Within this period, Indigenous resistance saw the emergence of the Aborigines' Progressive Association established by Bill Ferguson, William Cooper's petitioning of King George V to have Aboriginal representatives in parliament, and the publishing of the first Aboriginal monthly newspaper, the *Australian Abo Call* by Jack Patten. It proclaimed 26 January as 'The Day of Mourning' and it listed a ten-point plan that encompassed a call for rights, including raising the status of Aborigines to citizens under the Constitution. It also saw the first exhibition by Albert Namatjira. Evocative rich watercolour landscapes articulated the vibrancy and brilliance of the land through the eyes of an Indigenous person. In 1948 Australia became a signatory to the United Nations Declaration of Human Rights, in effect declaring itself as an international member state and subject to the responsibilities and obligations of upholding human rights—not only political and civil rights but also economic, social and cultural rights.

It was not until the 1967 referendum that discrimination against Aborigines was removed from the Constitution and

Indigenous people were accorded the rights inherent in being citizens of a nation-state. As the Aboriginal and Torres Strait Islander Commission said: 'Basic social rights such as the right to employment, education, training, a minimum income and access to basic health, housing and community services are integral to full participation and contribution to Australia's economic and social development'.[3] That it took some sixty-six years to become citizens of the Commonwealth is perhaps more indicative of the rate of change for any issues where Indigenous rights are concerned. Some thirty-four years later we are still trying to have those basic citizenship rights upheld. It is not so surprising, then, that the overturning of the legal fiction *terra nullius* took some two hundred years, and let me state categorically, it was at the behest of Indigenous people that these challenges were made.

The recognition of rights for Indigenous peoples is not only about the recognition of citizenship rights, but also about collective rights as indigenous people. Those rights reflect the provisions for protection against actions intending to deprive Indigenous peoples of their cultural integrity, and against integration and assimilation, and are concerned with the right to maintain, practise and revitalise cultural traditions. They are about the right of Indigenous people to a distinct identity and culture, including the right to control the education system and to educate in their own language. The state has had no interest in recognising and enshrining these rights; they have been dragged through history kicking and screaming.

During this period the Gurindji struck for their rights and began a seven-year battle for their land, while the federal government gave the Nabalco mining company a forty-two-year lease to mine bauxite at Yirrkala. In 1969 the Commonwealth Office of Aboriginal Affairs was established while the first Aboriginal delegation went to New York and presented a statement on the condition of Australian Aborigines to the office of the United Nations secretary-general.

The international arena is familiar to indigenous people or Australia. In 1971, with the first census taking place, the Northern Territory ruled in the Gove Land Rights case that Aborigines, under Australian law, did not own the Arnhem Land reserve, which effectively meant that Nabalco could mine there. The 1970s were an auspicious time: this period included the establishment of the Aboriginal Legal and Medical services, the election of the first indigenous member of parliament, Neville Bonner, and Evonne Goolagong's win at Wimbledon. But the proclamation of the Queensland Aborigines Act chartered how those living on reserves could have their culture and customs banned, their reading matter, mail, recreation, marital and sexual relationships censored; their work and wages decreased and people's movements recorded.

In 1972, the Tent Embassy was established on the lawns of Parliament House in Canberra and the world witnessed the actual brutality of the nation-state, with police clashes with Indigenous people screened across the world. The 1970s witnessed the rise of the land rights movement; Indigenous people challenged the right of state control over their homelands. In 1975, the Racial Discrimination Act came into force as the state enacted domestic legislation as a result of its international obligations under the International Convention on the Elimination of all Forms of Racial Discrimination.

The 1980s saw the consolidation of the Indigenous platform domestically and internationally—the quest for rights, the emergence of Indigenous art and culture, the Long March and the Bicentenary. In 1992 Australia suddenly took a huge step towards adulthood. Nurtured for some ten years, Eddie Mabo's quest for recognition of rights proved to be a legal high watermark for Australia. The historic decision of the High Court in its determinations of the Mabo case shook the foundations upon which Australians had maintained their power base and notions of supremacy. That the High Court overturned the legal fiction of *terra nullius* and recognised Indigenous property rights has reverberated throughout the 1990s. What a telling lesson about Australia's maturity and wisdom.

The enactment of the Native Title Act of 1993 and its assertion that freehold and leasehold grants extinguished native title was refuted by the decision of the High Court in *Wik* in 1996, whereby extinguishment was not guaranteed. This was swiftly followed by the 'Ten Point Plan' and the Native Title Amendment Bill in 1997 which sought to remove the right of Indigenous people to negotiate, and proposed extinguishment of native title. The Racial Discrimination Act served its polity well, as the state had to contend with the fact that it could not legislate actively against its citizens on the basis of race. We witnessed one of the most bitter power struggles between the state, the elites and Indigenous people.

We witnessed the vilification of Indigenous people, the Royal Commission into Aboriginal Deaths in Custody, the obscenity of mandatory sentencing on children, which has been loudly condemned, the denial and belittling of the experiences of the stolen generation, subjected to barbaric practices dismissive of the fundamental relationship between parent and progeny, the emergence of the ugly face of racism, the denigration of the judiciary entrusted with legal standards of our conduct towards one another; the megalomania of the state, the ignorance and confusion of the polity, the contempt of international bodies that determine global, moral and ethical standards for our coexistence as the mass of humanity, and the fear of a nation-state. What a telling lesson. Telling indeed.

And yet the restoration of Indigenous property rights enabled this country to move ahead. Indigenous people and pastoralists engaged in a dialogue and negotiated coexistence on the land by developing regional agreements; an inter-cultural dialogue where the interpretation of the world according to the subjective values of both Indigenous and non-Indigenous people can be accommodated. There is no dominant philosophy of interpretation. An oppositional and conflictual paradigm does not augur well for the concept of a united Australia—a nation that honours all its peoples. The accommodation of all Australian identities is paramount to nationhood as well as the premise that the nation upholds the rights of its members, rights that are assumed by many, but that are not enjoyed by Indigenous people *en masse*. Restitution is about recognising the present and ensuring that it reflects the maturity and wisdom we have garnered from our past.

Restitution requires measures that encompass prevention, education, protection and provision of effective remedies through the institutional and structural mechanisms of the state to ensure that all benefit through participation. According to ATSIC, restitution encompasses:

- self-determination and the ability and resources to develop Aboriginal and Torres Strait Islander communities on the basis of Indigenous knowledge and aspirations
- full equality of treatment for Indigenous Peoples
- recognition of their status as the Indigenous peoples and original owners of the land
- recognition and protection of Indigenous cultures
- compensation for dispossession
- equitable access to government programs
- adequate resources to overcome disadvantage; and
- recognition of Indigenous sovereignty.[4]

The reform required highlights the following priorities:

- major institutional and structural change, including constitutional reform and recognition, regional self-government and regional agreements, and the negotiation of a treaty or comparable document which must address the issue of compensation;
- overcoming inequities and inefficiencies in service delivery, including the achievement of genuine access and equity in Commonwealth, state/territory and local government programs and revised Commonwealth-state funding arrangements;
- full recognition of the social and cultural diversity of Aboriginal people and Torres Strait Islanders, and the need for policies and programs to have the flexibility to enable them to be tailored to address more effectively the varying local circumstances and priorities of Indigenous communities and groups;
- protection of rights through such means as recognition of customary laws, protection of intellectual and cultural property and recognition of Indigenous rights through a Bill of Rights;

- practical measures to enhance opportunities for economic development and to achieve objectives such as improved public awareness of Indigenous cultures and Indigenous issues.[5]

Concurrent are reconciliation and the national strategies to sustain the reconciliation process, promote recognition of Aboriginal and Torres Strait Islander rights, overcome disadvantage and aim for economic independence. In ten years we have witnessed the increasing awareness of the cultures, histories and rights of the first peoples of Australia. That reconciliation is now a people's movement in the twenty-first century augurs well for a future where we can discuss and debate in recognition of the fact that we shape our future. Today in Australia a great debate rages about the moral and ethical position of ourselves and the wider world. All these developments reveal that we as Australians have reached our Rubicon and we need to be aware of what that means for the future. There is no turning back. None of us can go back to the old order.

We are engaged in one of the most dynamic dialogues of our times. In its wake, old orders will be challenged and deconstructed and new orders will rise and permeate the landscape of our consciousness. This is the age of ethics. We are confronted by a convergence of issues so profound that we will need to rethink and reassess our place in the world and our relationships to one another, to negotiate the complex, interwoven and interdependent nature of our realities. Civil, political, economic, social, cultural, scientific, technological and environmental paradigms will require our considered, informed, moral and ethical responses—for each and every action there will be a consequence. For each and every paradigm, there will be impact. What we decide to do will shape the legacy for future generations of this century.

That legacy will be a result of ideas that manifest themselves in cultural, intellectual and spiritual action. We can provide a eucharist for humanity or play a game of cynical euchre. When we understand the nature of the events that are shaping us and the inherent philosophy informing them, we will reach an understanding as to what our path may be and how we can proceed down that path. It will take courage and leadership at a far more personal level than we have witnessed or assumed to date. It will take personal commitment—we must act the way we wish our society to become. If we acquiesce or abrogate our responsibility for involvement, we will bring into effect a society that we cannot shun, for we will have created it willingly through either our action or inaction. The personal is indeed the political.

Reconciliation is essentially about how we reconcile our past to our future in recognition of our diversity and our hopes for a shared future: a united Australia that respects this land of ours, values the Aboriginal and Torres Strait Islander heritage and provides justice and equity for all. How do we achieve a common standard by which we may begin to coexist and to realise a sense of nationhood in which our identity is a reflection of our culture? This, I believe, is the challenge for our imagination and in our actions, the realisation of our humanity.

Only you can know the depth of your commitment to the future. I for one want to know how far we shall journey in this time together as Australians.

Come, let us talk together about our future.

ENDNOTES

1. Oodgeroo Noonuccal, *My People*, Jacaranda Press, Melton, 1978.
2. Council for Aboriginal Reconciliation, 'Roadmap for Reconciliation, 2000'.
3. Aboriginal and Torres Strait Islander Commission, *Recognition, Rights and Reform: A Report to Government on Native Title Social Justice Measures*, 1996.
4. Aboriginal and Torres Strait Islander Commission, *Recognition, Rights and Reform: A Report to Government on Native Title Social Justice Measures* 1995, p. 12.
5. ibid., p. 12.

9

GREG CRAVEN

Similar diversity: The Australian states and the Australian nation

INTRODUCTION

At the very outset of this lecture, I am obliged to make a highly damaging confession: I have always been fond of the Australian States. This is so even though I hail from Victoria and as a boy was taught to regard the lesser populaces of the 'outlying' States with the sort of reverence usually reserved for three-day-old road kills. Of course, having been exiled to Western Australia at the advanced age of thirty-eight my previous eccentricities are now regarded as commendable insights. Drawing, therefore, on this rich blend of childhood perversity and Western Australian chauvinism, the essential thesis of this lecture will be that the States are far from superfluous components of Australian political and social culture. On the contrary, within the overall construct of Australian national identity, the States provide a genuine element of regional diversity, even on occasion an indispensable element of regional eccentricity, and to anyone who values diversity their continued existence is thus both defensible and desirable.

The states in Australian social and political mythology

This may be dealt with briefly. There can be few more disreputable positions in wider Australian political debate than that of a protagonist for the States. In polite intellectual circles, to be described as a 'centralist' means simply that one is sane. To be characterised as a 'States righter', on the other hand, is the equivalent of being branded the idiot natural son of former Queensland premier Sir Joh Bjelke-Petersen.

The emanations of this widespread intellectual disdain for the States are many but consistent. One of the most profound is that, so far as possible, the existence of the States is politely ignored. In my own field of law, for example, most Australians would believe without thinking that the Commonwealth is the dominant Australian lawmaker. Yet if any of us were to be run over in a Sydney street it would be the laws of New South Wales on traffic, dangerous driving, hospitals and (sadly) funeral parlours that would matter.

Examples of such determined ignorance of the States could be multiplied almost endlessly. What they reveal is that many Australians have an obsession with the national and something approaching a guilty shame for anything connected merely with a State. Thus, we revel in terms like 'national broadcaster', 'national companies', 'national media outlets', 'national sport' and 'national character': Indeed, at times, the adjective 'national' preceding any given noun seems little more than our substitute term for 'really good'. 'State', by way of contrast, connotes small, parochial and nasty.

A connected tendency is to deny the diversity of the States, maintaining that there really are no differences between them and that their separate existence is thus irrational and beneath notice. A recurrent theme is that the old colonial limits, upon which the boundaries of the States are based, were mere accidents of history, and that those States therefore possess no genuine historic personality. All of this has given rise to one of the great pipe dreams of Australian political thought: namely, that the States might usefully be abolished in favour of a unitary nation. This view was expressed during the Federation debates themselves by such New South Welsh politicians as Sir George Dibbs, who felt that the sister colonies might most profitably be absorbed within the warm embrace of their mother, New South Wales. Ever since, abolition of the States has been the recurrent desideratum of Commonwealth governments although, since the passing of the Whitlam government, the guilty fantasies of the Commonwealth seem to have focused less upon the prospect of actually abolishing the States than on cutting them up into smaller, more co-operative 'regional' governments.

Reasons for hostility towards the States

There are strong grounds to suspect that one of the primary reasons for the general disrepute of the States is that their existence is seen by many as inconsistent with what might be referred to as Australia's coalescing national epic. According to this view, the single defining moment of Australian political history was Federation, which involved a coming together of the disparate political parts of Australia into a single whole. As a consequence, anything that stresses this heroic wholeness must by definition be good, while anything that reminds us of past divergence—such as the States as successors to the old colonies—correspondingly must be bad.

A related view is that the existence of the States is both historically and theoretically inconsistent with any genuine notion of national progress. The idea here essentially is that the States invariably constitute barriers to the achievement of the good ideas of the central government, are probably internally corrupt and certainly hamper every conceivable form of economic advancement. This almost invariably leads on to the fundamental proposition that if only all power could be centralised in the Commonwealth government, all Australia's problems would be magically solved.

The cause of the States is not helped by the fact that their very existence is seriously out of tune with the reality of Australia's contemporary power centres. The point here is that the States are, by definition, disaggregated and disseminated. They include not merely powerful, estimable, serious places like Melbourne/Victoria and Sydney/New South Wales, but also places that every journalist, advertising executive and boutique lawyer knows are deeply irrelevant, such as Tasmania and South Australia. Not surprisingly, then, the Australia of the 2000s as seen on national television news, is an Australia designed in their own image by that nation's foci of influence, and includes none of these backward appendages.

Of course, there also exist more fundamental causes for the hostility on the part of a wide swathe of Australians towards the States. One is that Australians seem to have a difficulty in juggling two communal identities. Certainly, many Australians display deep suspicion towards any of their co-citizens who confess to such a dualistic identity, that is, as an Australian and (say) a Queenslander. To such monotypical Australians this dualism of communal identity is internally inconsistent and even threatening. This is very different from the position that tends to apply within many other federations. Nevertheless, in the eyes of a large proportion of Australians, particularly those from the great eastern population centres, for a fellow citizen to say that they are 'a Queenslander' or 'a Western Australian' in any other tones than those of hushed apology constitutes a direct challenge to the coherence of the nation. In response to any unrepentant hillbillies bold enough to utter such national heresy the stern reproof quickly will be delivered: 'No—you are an Australian'. Yet the question has to be: why cannot one be both?

What all this strongly suggests is the subsistence of a certain national insecurity on the part of many Australians. One might even hazard the profoundly unpalatable thesis that an Australian national identity seems to be insufficiently established for its guardians lightly to tolerate anything that might be regarded as a rival communal loyalty, and this may partly explain the intense hostility felt by some Australian 'nationalists' to the States.

Indeed, it often seems that deep within the Australian political tradition exists something of an historic antipathy to internal diversity and to the extent that the States represent precisely such a deviant sub-national element they are the natural objects of that antipathy. One reason our wider political tradition embodies such tendencies is simple: that tradition is profoundly English. Thus, when one strips the constitutional history of England of its trimmings, and above all its self-congratulation, there emerges from among such golden threads as parliamentary democracy and the rule of law another strong but far less shining strand: the ruthless, progressive, single-minded centralisation of power in the sovereign parliament at Westminster and the equally grim suppression of any countervailing tendency, chiefly as represented by the various Celtic remnants of the British Isles. In the local Australian translation, this privileging of ever-expanding central hegemony is profoundly inconsistent with the notion of semi-independent regionalism represented by the States.

All of this is compounded, perhaps, by something of a national characteristic not to discern differences that, rather than being of small significance, are nevertheless significant in their smallness. In many ways we are a nation with a talent for the obvious. We celebrate a big country, a big sun, big oceans and loud cricketers. Many of us are intolerant of the subtle. Consequently, in assessing whether differences exist between the States, we are inclined to look for blindingly obvious differences. When we have to deal with the subtler, smaller, softer differences, we are inclined to dismiss them as trivial or simply non-existent.

Finally, there is what might be referred to as the factor of the pathetic. Put simply, everybody likes to be on the side of a winner, and the Australian States have been among the most dedicated of losers in recent Australian history. Over the last hundred years the States have lost all but the rags of their financial and constitutional independence. Not surprisingly, therefore, there is a strong and accurate perception within Australia that the States are in inexorable decline, and in a nation that values success they have all the kudos of the serial loser.

The diversity of the States

One may begin on a note that is undeniably light-hearted, but intriguing nonetheless. It is strikingly peculiar that, in a nation supposedly dedicated to the proposition that there is no difference between its States, an overwhelming majority of the national population apparently subscribes with enthusiasm to highly negative stereotypes of the inhabitants of all the States other than that in which they themselves reside. Thus to all but themselves Victorians are arrogant; Queenslanders are slow; Western Australians are rednecks; South Australians are whingers; Tasmanians are either parochial or inbred, depending upon one's degree of charity. Finally, in the case of the New South Welsh, I regret to inform them that they are shallow, uncultured, glitzy and obsessed with money. No one is suggesting that these stereotypes are true or profound, but they undeniably exist.

The second and much more significant point concerning the diversity of the States is obvious but often ignored. As a matter of brute reality, there genuinely is more to Australia than Sydmelberra. We need regularly to remind ourselves that the south-eastern corner of Australia represents a tiny part of its total land mass, displays an unrepresentative range of climatic conditions, sustains only a very small relative proportion of Australia's indigenous species and is host only to a very limited number of Australia's indigenous languages. Outside this coastal corner there are, incredibly, millions of people who not only do not listen to John Laws, but have neither a negative nor positive opinion about him. For the overwhelming majority of these outlanders it was financially impossible to go anywhere near the Sydney Olympics, and to these people the Melbourne Cricket Ground on grand final day represents nothing more than a flickering television image. Things are different out there.

Again, it is always said that Australia is a highly urbanised country, and this is often offered in partial support of our supposed national uniformity. Our degree of urbanisation is undeniable, but outside its south-eastern corner Australia is urbanised in a way different from that which applies in Sydmelberra. Australians living beyond the south-eastern seaboard do not live in the vast megametropoli so familiar to the residents of Sydney or Melbourne, but in town-cities like Adelaide and Perth (and even Brisbane) where life undoubtedly is slower, but even more significantly, where citizens are much more intimately connected to a wide range of their co-residents.

Of course, all these points are simply aspects of a single fundamental truth. The incontrovertible truth is that there exists a vast diversity of conditions between the States. This is an uncongenial fact that is extremely easy to ignore if one never leaves Sydmelberra, but speaking as an ethnic Victorian, to stand in the vast Kimberley region of Western Australia is to realise how very wrong one is. There, one's immediate thought is not, 'This is another place', or even, 'This is another state', but rather, 'This is another country'.

Taking Western Australia, then, as arguably the best but certainly to me the most familiar example of any 'outlying State', it is readily apparent that its character is shaped by many factors largely unknown to other Australians. A hard example is comprised in the position of Aboriginal people in Western Australia. Obviously, Aboriginal people are disadvantaged throughout the Commonwealth. However, in addition to their shared disadvantage, the circumstances of Western Australia's Aboriginal people differ greatly from the circumstances of most of the Aboriginal population of Victoria or New South Wales. Compared to, say, Victoria, Western Australia has a relatively large Aboriginal population, including a large number of broadly disseminated rural communities that have heroically maintained strong elements of their culture and their law, many of which are located in desert or arid areas remote from Perth. These are important facts that are highly divergent from any south-eastern norm.

Indeed, the realities surrounding Aboriginal people seem to constitute a basic differential truth between States like Western Australia (and possibly Queensland) and the states of the south-eastern bloc. Put bluntly, in Western Australia it is not possible to ignore Aboriginal people, either as individuals or as a social phenomenon. This simply has not been true for many European Australians living in States like Victoria. There, while one knows that Aborigines exist, and while one now intellectually knows that reconciliation and land rights are important issues, there is no necessary occasion to see, meet, speak to or engage with Aboriginal people, who are therefore too often treated as concepts or issues rather than human beings. In Western Australia, however, one must encounter Aboriginal people within one's own life on an everyday basis. What this means is that, for good or ill, the character of a Western Australian partly is that of an individual who has had to take personal account of Aboriginal people, whether as racist or reconciliator.

Of course, some of the most profound differences between seemingly similar communities are often the most subtle. Pursuing this vein of the subtly significant, one of the most fundamental relationships possessed by a human being is with their country, using 'country' in this sense not as some abstraction of the nation-state, but much more profoundly as denoting the very particular physical place in which one lives and which in turn lives in one. In Australia at the most trivial level, this notion of country involves very real differences in the everyday life of Australians from different states.

Thus, to dwell quite literally on the surface, it is a plain fact that climatically privileged Western Australians and Queenslanders tend to wear fewer clothes than Victorians. Similarly, Western Australian and Queensland children tend to swim more and better than their Victorian and Tasmanian counterparts. To Western Australian children, those cuddly bush staples of Australian children's literature the platypus and the koala, utterly absent from any WA forest, are as immediately relevant as the tiger and the hippopotamus. A Victorian may kid herself that she lives in a 'big country', but a Western Australian or a Queenslander really does. Not surprisingly, Western Australians have a profoundly different idea of distance from Victorians and New South Welshmen.

Nearer the core of the matter, one encounters within Australia pastel-hued differences that nevertheless arguably represent genuine divergences in State aesthetic. One of the most subtle of these falls into the category of what might be described as 'atmospheric memory'. To human beings memory is one of the most powerful of all forces, serving to locate them within the ever-changing mist of time and circumstance. Very often, memory is attached not merely to a perception of time, but to an intense feeling of place and surrounding. Thus as a Melburnian I have always been aware that Victoria's most delightful season is autumn, a time when one, like Keats, quite seriously could talk of mists and mellow fruitfulness. Yet the harsh reality is that Western Australia has no autumn, and therefore its people share no romance of autumn.

Similarly, I always have been struck by Donald Horne's observation in *The Education of Young Donald* that in his garden, his grandfather had planted his memories around him. This thought seems very effectively to express the idea of the intimate relationship between individuality and the creation or adoption of a personal landscape, whether through the manufacture of an artificial entity such as garden, or through an emotional commitment to a natural landscape. Coming myself from Victoria, my childhood is filled with recollections of daphne, daffodils, fuchsias and forget-me-nots. Yet having valiantly attempted to plant these memories around me in Perth, they have quite unforgivably died. Plants are far more honest organisms than people and they are inclined to testify biologically to the truth that Western Australia and Victoria are indeed very different, in much the same way that the misplanted crops of the early settlers bluntly informed them that they were in the Antipodes, not Surrey.

Of course, no discussion of matters such as these would be complete without mention being made of that great Australian obsession, sport, where difference reigns supreme. It is, for example, true that Australia is notionally 'united' by a single cricket team, but as anyone who follows the game will know, selection to that team in the first instance continues to depend on a player's performance in the competition among the States and there is rarely a significant period of commentary during a Test match broadcast where reference was not made to the State origin of this or that Australian cricketer. An even more obvious point of State division is football. The 'southern' States of Victoria, South Australia, Tasmania and Western Australia play the code of football employed by God and his Archangels, while the 'northern States'—New South Wales and its dupe, Queensland—futilely scratch away at Rugby League. Naturally, this division between codes is supplemented by manic State rivalries within those codes. To behold 40,000 Western Australians spontaneously maintaining absolute silence when a Victorian team kicks a goal at Subiaco oval is to witness one of the world's great phenomena of concerted mass inaction, inspired by a passionately held sense of difference.

Earlier in this lecture I lightheartedly posited the existence of State stereotypes. Similarly, it is difficult not to accept that particular prominent personalities only could have emerged in their home States. For example, how could Sir Joh Bjelke-Petersen be imagined other than as a Queenslander? Again, could Jeff Kennett have lurched to eminence on the political scene anywhere other than Victoria, with that eclectic mix of arrogance, third-grade aristocratic hauteur, gung-ho business rapacity, genuine State patriotism and an appalling haircut? Going further back in our history, Menzies was, profoundly, desperately Victorian; Evatt fundamentally New South Welsh; Downer unmistakably a South Australian; and Deakin and Isaacs too hyperactively self-assured to be anything other than from Victoria. Barton was just too fond of pleasure to hail from anywhere but Sydney.

There are, of course, arguments against the existence of genuine difference between the States. One is that as between New South Wales and Victoria, the behemoths of the Australian federation, there exists no real degree of State divergence, on the grounds that any palpable difference arises rather between the great cities of Melbourne and Sydney than between their host States. Yet the reality is that both these States are so dominated by their respective capitals that they closely resemble city-states bestriding their associated hinterlands, so that to a very large extent the difference between the capitals is the same thing as the difference between the States.

Another argument against the diversity of the States is that our nation's true line of division runs between the city and the bush rather than between the States. However, the existence of an additional line of division among Australians hardly constitutes a refutation of State diversity. In any event, there is a very significant correlation between this urban–rural divide and the diversity encountered among the States. One of the things that makes Queensland as an entity so significantly different from small, highly urbanised Victoria, and from rather larger but still highly urban New South Wales, is the existence and influence of its vast and varied rural districts and associated provincial towns, while the immense rural expanses of Western Australia operate to similar effect.

Probably the most common retort to the assertion of any significant degree of diversity among the States is that because their boundaries are 'artificial', they have no real, as opposed to merely constitutional, existence. In the first place, this argument tends to assume that boundaries between national and sub-national entities are usually determined rationally, and that such an exercise is a precondition to the development of a distinct identity. This is hardly the case, as most Europeans and South Americans would testify. Secondly, it ignores the salient fact that the boundaries of the Australian States, however imperfect in their inception, have had about 150 years to develop validity. Victoria, for example, mercifully separated from New South Wales in 1850, and thus has had 151 years in which to practise its role as a distinct political and social community. This is a period significantly longer than the lifespan of many nation-states in a constantly changing world, certainly far longer than the duration of the average national constitution. Finally, attacks on the adequacy of State boundaries do not reflect the reality that, while some of their features are highly artificial, most are perfectly plausible. Broken Hill conceivably could be in South Australia. Broome is as surely in the West as Launceston is in Tasmania.

Similarly overstated is the proposition that the marvels of modern technology have so shortened physical and psychological distances between the States that they have effectively dissolved State boundaries and differences. Perhaps the most lauded example is that of speedy air travel between the States. This argument might have a certain plausibility until one lives in Western Australia and appreciates precisely what 'fast' air travel over the vast continent of Australia actually means, with profoundly incompatible time zones, schizophrenic weather conditions and hopelessly tangled connections. What seals the issue is the sagging realisation that, in the supposedly unified Australia of the twenty-first century, it is actually not possible to fly direct from Perth to the alleged national capital of Canberra. Of course, the whole argument must be moot to the vast bulk of Australians who are not part of the social elite to whom air travel is an almost daily occurrence.

The final denial of State diversity is the assertion that it is logically inconceivable for citizens not to have abandoned their State identities in favour of a single, undifferentiated national allegiance. Yet within many societies citizens have several dimensions of social identity, which are in no sense mutually exclusive. Thus it is perfectly possible for a president of San Antonio to be an American, a Texan and an Hispanic American, and for each of those identities to reinforce the other. This hardly should come as a shock in Australia, where multiculturalism has shown us that it is perfectly possible to be Australian and Irish, Australian and Vienamese, Australian and Italian, and Australian and anything else. Why in heaven's name can someone not be Australian, Lebanese and a Queenslander?

A DEFENCE OF THE STATES

As creatures of diversity, the States may be defended on aesthetic, constitutional and functional grounds. Very briefly, in terms of aesthetics, it already has been demonstrated that the States are indeed diverse, and the assertion is now made that civic diversity is a force for good within the nation-state. Self-evidently, the richness of many national cultures and characters around the world has depended significantly upon the contributions of their diverse regions. Or to put it another way, much of the eccentricity of nations depends upon this interplay of internal diversity, and in a homogeneous world we are all in desperate need of eccentricity. This proposition surely would ring true to a citizen of France, Italy, the United Kingdom or the United States.

It is indeed curious that at a time when we rightly celebrate multiculturalism for the sheer variety that it brings to human life in Australia, so many of us are so reluctant to admit to the existence of any degree of diversity in the States. Moreover, at a time when so many of us share a deep nervousness about the creeping lava of Los Angeles popular culture and its ghastly, supranational homogeneity, we surely should cherish any element of our own national diversity.

Turning to a constitutional and functional defence of the States, one should commence with the brutal fact that Australia is intrinsically and irreversibly federal—that is, a society inextricably organised around the existence of State communities. Obviously, this reality flows in a purely legal way from the Constitution, but in a far deeper sense the sheer fact of Australian federalism would not change were the States to be abolished tomorrow. The reason for this is that virtually every element of Australian life is configured upon the existence of the States, and this would not change were the States themselves to cease to be as legal organisms. On the contrary, everything from football to kennel clubs, education, dioceses of churches, distribution of newspapers and the organisation of political parties would continue to follow the old State boundaries. The fact is that after one hundred years of Federation the Australian political and social genius is a federal genius. Indeed, it is worth pausing for a moment to imagine what precisely the abolition of the States would be likely to achieve as a matter of administrative and political reality. The blunt answer, presumably, would be a federal bureaucracy greatly enlarged to take up all the old State functions, organised upon State lines.

This conclusion is not affected by the fact that the Constitution itself, considered purely as a vehicle for the protection of the States, has undoubtedly been something of a dismal failure. This diagnosis is made notwithstanding the undoubted fact that the founders collectively were ardent State protagonists. There is an idea abroad that those who wrote the Australian Constitution embraced federalism only because they faced no practical alternative. Yet the best of the founders—Barton, Deacon, Griffith and O'Connor—were motivated by high considerations of principle, guided by the far-from-pedestrian writings of Jefferson, Madison, Hamilton and Bryce. This principled basis for Australian federalism and its component States is as valid today as it was in 1900.

In the first place, we need to understand federalism as a geographic analogy to the principle of the separation of powers. Just as this principle prevents any one individual or organism from gaining total hegemony across the different components of our constitutional apparatus, so federalism ensures its own cohesive set of checks and balances on a geographic basis. The fundamental result of federalism thus is that no person or institution can simultaneously achieve political, social or even intellectual suzerainty over every portion of Australian society at the same time.

Moreover, in functional terms, the inherent effect of federalism is that whenever extreme measures are advocated anywhere in Australia—including Canberra—there will exist elsewhere a strong, organised policy critique of those measures. Undeniably, the operation of such a process is expensive, time-consuming and (in some senses) inefficient. Yet much the same may be said for the separation of powers, judicial independence and democracy itself. Given our unquestioning and entirely appropriate respect for such concepts, it is striking how intolerant many of us are of our one great constitutional check and balance that has had the misfortune to be expressed in a regional rather than a national idiom.

In this connection, it is sometimes suggested that the abolition of the States and their replacement by regional governments would dissolve the alleged inefficiencies of the States, while preserving intact all virtues of the federal dimension. In fact, any such step would utterly destroy Federation's geographic separation of powers. Thus, in order that sub-national governments may constitute restraining centres of power and influence, they must enjoy a certain 'constitutional mass'. What this means, in effect, is that they must at the very least be free of the threat of abolition by any overweening central authority.

This is the case in Australia, where the States could be abolished only by a referendum to amend the Constitution, which would in fact have to be passed not only by a national majority, but also by a majority in every State. Regional governments are not usually so constitutionally secure, and typically a central government will possess the power to dismiss a regional administration, or even to reconstitute a region itself. This is one reason why the concept of regional government has been so appealing to successive Commonwealth leaders.

A further claim for the States centres on their role as guardians of popular democracy. The essence of this claim is that, as governmental systems, they are necessarily much closer to their regional populations than any national government, thus better understanding the problems and conditions of their territories and being more responsive to the desires of their populations. The degree of physical proximity between State administrations and their populations necessarily advantages them in this sense over their national counterpart. Thus, in contemplating the position of a State such as Western Australia within the policy matrix of the Australian federation, some hard questions need to be addressed. First, why would Canberra understand the issues of Western Australia? What knowledge of local conditions does Canberra have? What insight can it claim? Above all, what interest does it even have in such matters?

Another fundamental question is even more stark. If Canberra did happen to understand the issues that engage Western Australia, why would it care what the population of that State thought about those issues? Political logic dictates that to Canberra, issues concerning Western

Australia should be resolved according to the wishes of the majority of the Australian people as a whole, not the wishes of the people of Western Australia. It is thus a simple fact, wholesome or otherwise, that State governments will in general terms be closer to and more representative of State populations than the national government. A useful test of this is to imagine the position of the smaller States within totally unified Australia. What capacity would the populations of Western Australia or South Australia have to make their voice meaningfully heard on issues that were highly particular to their State, but highly contentious nationally?

Of course, the proximity of State governments to their populations necessarily carries with it costs as well as benefits. Some would respond to the proposition that the States are conceptual bastions of popular democracy with horrendous accounts of the Queensland gerrymanders of Sir Joh Bjelke-Petersen. Yet while these undoubtedly muted the voice of the people of Queensland, the abolition of Queensland would by definition silence that voice as the means of expressing the views of that State's population as a distinct, independent, organised collectivity.

A more contemporary spin on the notion of the States as popular democracies would be to conceive of them as communities, groups of people with common bonds, based partly upon mutual interests but also upon some deeper feeling of shared identity. Over the past ten years it has become very clear that Australians desire community: they are intensely nervous of being reduced to undifferentiated economic units of a depressingly rational whole. Australian governments are increasingly finding that to treat these desires as irrational—whether in the context of shires, schools or hospitals—is a fatal error. In short, people desperately desire connections that operate below the megalevel of a shared common citizenship in some remote nation-state, and the States are a fundamental part of this feeling. This is particularly true in the outlying States where it is not physically possible for Australians to fully partake in a Sydmelberran version of Australian identity.

There also is something to be said for the idea that the States serve as useful social laboratories, experimenting with a range of policy options before any one is held to have proved itself worthy of adoption on some wider level. Of this tendency, there are some unlikely but telling examples. Thus, the current mandatory sentencing debate, with the unwelcome attention that it has attracted to Western Australia and the Northern Territory, is in the long run less likely to illustrate the capacity of 'rogue States' to adopt inappropriate policy initiatives than the capacity of our federal system to isolate and demonstrate the uselessness of such measures before they are more generally adopted.

There also exist innumerable positive examples where the successful initiative of one State is adopted by others, or even by the Commonwealth. For example, in the field of justice, the Commonwealth has just reorganised its system of tribunals in line with Victorian reforms. In terms of 'work in progress', the law regarding the thorny social issue of prostitution embodies a variety of approaches among the States. One, or an amalgam of several, eventually will prove superior, and be absorbed on a wider basis, with each State having due regard to its own special circumstances.

In this context we need to understand that the sheer area of law and policy under the command of the States gives them a constant opportunity to innovate and that the products of such innovation may command a wide audience. At a time when we pore over every international treaty for its Australian implications it is not widely appreciated that the policy initiatives of the despised Australian States are routinely and respectfully considered by reforming governments in such places as the United Kingdom, Canada and even the United States.

Naturally, the response to these hopeful examples from those who wish to see an end of the States is to ask about atrocities, stolen children, and the denial of land rights and mandatory sentencing. These are weighty issues; if we are to attack the records of the States upon issues of human rights, where does the Commonwealth stand? Who was the author of the White Australia policy? How do we view the Constitution's own treatment of Aboriginal people? Has our approach to internment of aliens and refugees over the past century been acceptable? These are not cheap shots, but simply make it very clear that the happy notion that the central government of Australia necessarily has a monopoly on political morality is fatuous and naïve. They also point us to a fundamental issue. Assuming that no State governments existed and that a unitary, omnicompetent national government decided to implement on a universal basis any of the State policies that they have so reviled, what would be the position?

THE FUTURE OF THE STATES

Whatever else may be true, the States will not go away. The old Labor dream of abolition has faded, if only because of referendum requirements. In any event, as has been argued here, even were the States to be abolished they would continue to exist in geographic, political and social reality. The real constitutional threat to the States, therefore, is not one of assassination, but of continuing, gradual, debilitating decline.

One interesting question concerns the possible costs Australia might already have paid for its historical intolerance of internal diversity as represented by the States. Tentatively, our almost pathological antipathy to elements of diversity generated within our own Australian polity seems to make it harder for us to deal creatively with the demands of Aboriginal people for a qualified degree of self-government. The same cry that we are 'all Australians, all the same', so profoundly hostile to the States, is readily called up against a limited recognition of tribal law or local indigenous self-government. More certainly, our intolerance of internal diversity has greatly hindered any prospect of union between Australia and New Zealand. Had the Australian States been fostered since Federation and their constitutional positions substantially maintained, it would have been conceivable that a wary New Zealand might pay the reasonable price of entry into the federation. Yet how could New Zealand now contemplate the prospect of becoming merely another prisoner dragged behind the chariot of the Commonwealth? Undoubtedly, there will be great changes among the States over the next thirty years, many of which seem predictable. The battle between New South Wales and Victoria for the title of the 'Premier State' is at last over and New South Wales (and its metropolis Sydney) has won. This means that Sydney is and will continue to be the real capital of Australia, and that accordingly Sydney and New South Wales will dominate the

Australian federation. Victoria, the historic powerhouse of that federation, will almost certainly decline. Many of its traditional industries are under threat and Melbourne's status as the nation's business capital has waned. Like the deserted cities of the Incas, it seems less likely that Victoria will be sacked than increasingly forgotten.

Queensland should thrive. It is close to Sydney, richly resourced, and in the leisure age it is fashioned by God for leisure. Indeed, Queensland may come to surpass Victoria as a supporting act to New South Wales. Western Australia will continue to be an enigma, basking as a semi-independent grand duchy on the edge of Australia, though if it can ever harness effectively its natural wealth, deal creatively with the horrors of distance and conquer its own people's sun-stroked diffidence, The West may emerge as the new talent among the Australian States. As for South Australia and Tasmania, they will make even Victoria in the years of its modest decline seem a hive of industry and innovation.

But in ten, twenty, or eighty years, winners or losers, the States will never, ever be the same as each other. They will still be quirky, cranky and diverse. They still, for good or ill, will hold up and sometimes frustrate whatever the transient nationalism of the day lays down as national imperatives. They will still experiment with really good and really appalling policy ideas. Above all, they will continue to demonstrate the marvellous genius of the Australian people, as citizens of the States, for small, insignificant, subtle, rich, enhancing and vital difference. As an Australian, as a Victorian, and—heaven help me—as a half-Western Australian, I rejoice in that reality.

10

Helen Irving

Australia's constitutional identity: A conundrum for the 21st century

What do we see when we look in our constitutional mirror? Is it a familiar face, one we know well and have known for many years? A reflection that speaks to us of a long and useful lifetime, its features clear and instantly recognisable? Or do we stare at it and find only something bewildering, like the face of a friend from the distant past whose features are so altered with age that we have trouble being certain it is really the same person?

The centenary of Federation is surely a suitable time to ask such questions, a good moment to clear away the dust and have a peep. Perhaps we will like the old face, perhaps we won't care one way or another. But, one hundred years after the Australian Commonwealth began functioning, we owe it to ourselves to look long, even hard. The mirror is not yet cracked, the silver is not yet gone beyond repair, but we may be surprised—indeed, dismayed—at what we find, or fail to find, looking back at us.

Once upon a time, in the beginning, Australians looked in the mirror and saw themselves as the fairest of all. By 1901, after close to five decades of imagining a constitution and ten years of building one, they were exhilarated. In the words of South Australian premier Charles Kingston, an uncompromising radical democrat, it was 'the most magnificent Constitution into which the chosen representatives of a free and enlightened people have ever breathed the life of popular sentiment and national hope'.[1] As they celebrated the inauguration of the Commonwealth, those same free and enlightened people agreed, finding it a sublime and glorious instrument, a charter of democratic citizenship, a beacon for the future of world democracy. I am speaking of the same Constitution that we have inherited almost unchanged from that time. What was going on?

We can safely assume that Australians at the turn of the nineteenth century were not so dissimilar to ourselves that they actually got worked up over something that was objectively little more than a conveyancing contract or a grocer's bill. These were the High Victorians, after all. They were not familiar with modern art. They were not attuned to splashes of paint on canvas or techno music or minimalist poetry. They loved stories and decoration and colour and drama, and what we now find excessively sentimental poetry. Yet they thought the Constitution 'poetic'.

It is true that £6,000 was spent on champagne for the

celebrations of the inauguration of the Commonwealth in Sydney alone. *The Bulletin*, with typical irreverence, depicted the 'dawn of the Commonwealth' as a bunch of politicians waking up in Centennial Park on 2 January 1901 with a massive hangover. But, the national exuberance was not a matter of national inebriation.

The Constitution included, indeed, some of the most democratic provisions in the world at the time. Both Houses of parliament were to be directly elected. There was a ban on plural voting in Commonwealth elections. Members of parliament were to be paid a salary. Deadlocks between the two houses would be solved by going to the people. The referendum would serve as the means of constitutional change. This Constitution, said the Victorian liberal democrat Alfred Deakin, was 'vastly more liberal than any of the Constitutions under which we at present live.'[2]

The Constitution's preamble spoke of an 'indissoluble federal Commonwealth'. The name had been chosen at the first Federal Convention, in Sydney in 1891, to suggest the *common weal* or common good, and to remind people that this was the purpose of the union. The word 'indissoluble', it was thought, would avoid the danger of civil war. The federal system would respect the autonomy and distinctive identity of the states. The preamble also spoke of those federating as 'humbly relying on the blessing of Almighty God'. Contrary to what is sometimes claimed today, these words were chosen, said their mover, the Roman Catholic South Australian delegate, Patrick Glynn, as 'simple and unsectarian [,] ... expressive of ... the great elemental truth upon which all our creeds are based, and towards which the lines of our faiths converge'. They will, he said, 'thus become the pledge of religious toleration'.[3]

The Constitution had been written by delegates elected to the 1897–1898 Australasian Federal Convention. This Convention, as with the first in 1891, was open to the press and the public. Its work was reported and debated, and subjected to public criticism. At its completion, copies of the Constitution were sent to the electors. The Constitution was then approved by a referendum in each of the colonies, and only then was it adopted by the parliaments. This participatory process was unique and the people of the time knew it. It rested on a principle of democratic trust that we would find hard to improve upon today.

This is, I stress, the very same Constitution that we now believe to be so dull and pedestrian, that many find alien and some regard as democratically, even morally deficient. Certainly—like every other functioning federal constitution—it contains many 'businesslike' provisions. Certainly in style it is very different from what we might write today. But there is no evidence—despite what is sometimes claimed—that it was the product of a deliberate strategy on the part of any one group to accommodate its members' particular interests. The Constitution was written in response to a wide range of interests and wishes. People knew and understood the debates, and when they looked at the completed product, they saw in it almost nothing that they did not recognise.

This is not the case one hundred years later. Where the Constitution would have made sense to the majority in 1901, it is probably unintelligible to most Australians in 2001. I don't mean unintelligible because the vast majority has never seen it, let alone read it. I mean, even if they had seen it—indeed, *particularly* if they had seen it.

There are a number of reasons for this historical shift in

understanding, and, one hopes, an equal number of solutions.

At the time it was written, certain sections in the Constitution were intended to be purely transitional, operating only during the first couple of years or so of the Commonwealth. They were included because it was necessary to make interim arrangements for certain things while the colonies underwent their metamorphosis into states.

Secondly, Australia's relations with Britain have undergone many changes since 1901, and a range of sections which refer to the old imperial ties are no longer operative. The Empire—once a great and familiar idea to Australians—is scarcely remembered, let alone understood.

Thirdly, many of the institutions the Constitution creates and authorises are described in confusing and even misleading ways. What they do say depends upon a body of unwritten conventions and lies largely 'between the lines'. This was probably better understood in the past than it is now.

Fourthly, many of the issues of the nineteenth century are not those of today. The Constitution, among other things, distributes powers to make laws between the levels of government. It gives the Commonwealth powers over 'national' matters and in theory at least, leaves the rest to the state parliaments. What was thought of as 'national' one hundred years ago may not be what we think of as national today, and vice versa.

In addition to all this—not a flaw in the Constitution itself, but a difficulty in the context—we are surrounded by American movies and courtroom dramas that reinforce the idea that constitutions are declarations of great and passionate sentiment or that they necessarily contain a Fifth

Amendment. Even otherwise educated commentators confuse the United States Constitution with the Declaration of Independence or the ten amendments that make up the 'Bill of Rights' with the whole United States Constitution. They conclude that Australia's is not a real constitution and that the means of rectifying this national deficiency is simply to put in references to values or rights.

Genuine and merited as was the sentiment surrounding the Constitution's birth in 1901, we cannot restore our faith in it merely by telling and re-telling the historical story. The Constitution was an example of best practice in its time and the work of its framers makes an inspiring story, but so does the Magna Carta. Understanding the story is important—among other things, it saves us from making absurd claims or reinventing the wheel—but understanding the Constitution is more important.

What is to be done? First—the easy part—remove the detritus, those transitional sections that, without controversy, have no further currency in anyone's eyes. Send them to a constitutional elephants' graveyard for historians like myself to lament. Who, for example, would seriously cling to section 88, that tells us that '[u]niform duties of customs shall be imposed within two years after the establishment of the Commonwealth'? Or that part of Section 128 that says of proposed amendments to the Constitution: 'until the qualification of electors of members of the House of Representatives becomes uniform throughout the Commonwealth, only one-half the electors voting for and against the proposed law [to alter the Constitution] shall be counted in any State in which adult suffrage prevails'? In other words, if there was a referendum before the Commonwealth Franchise Act was passed, those states in which women had the vote were required to divide their number of votes by two, and count only one half.

This little provision is an important historical artefact, recording a time when women did not have the vote across the colonies, and when this was thought of as a dilemma raher than an invitation for all women to be granted the vote. But it has had no currency for many years. The first Commonwealth Franchise Act was passed in mid 1902, creating a uniform federal franchise, four years before the first referendum was held.

There is a significant number of other such sections. On its own, the historical record is not a good enough reason to retain them. If it were, we should have hung onto Section 127, removed by referendum in 1967, that said: 'in reckoning the numbers of the people of the Commonwealth . . . aboriginal natives shall not be counted'.

Now move to the dead wood, those sections that were once living, but are now obsolete because changes have taken place in Australia's constitutional relations with Britain over the twentieth century. Section 58, for example, discusses the procedure whereby the governor-general may 'reserve' his assent to a parliamentary Bill 'for the Queen's pleasure' and, in the event that he has assented to a Bill but she subsequently does not find it pleasing, Section 59 tells us that she may disallow the relevant law within one year. These sections were once the key to an empire in which domestic autonomy for the self-governing colonies was balanced with British control over foreign policy and with the principle of 'paramount force' of certain British statutes.

Since the passage of the Statute of Westminster in 1931 (or more precisely, since Australia ratified the Statute in

1942, backdating it to 1939), the Queen can no longer disallow an Act of the Australian parliament, and the governor-general has nowhere to take a 'reserved' Bill, even if he were inclined to reserve it. There are a number of similar dead branches on the constitutional tree, and we will probably have some argument about which to lop and which to leave. But one can be confident that agreement could be reached on much of the pruning.

The next step is to identify those sections of the Constitution that should be rewritten or new sections that should be included, in order to give an accurate description of our fundamental democratic practices. These practices are neither temporary nor obsolete. They are indeed the core of our constitutional framework for a democratic polity, and as such they should be stated clearly, not merely inferred. To persist with our gardening metaphor, we are lifting the rootball of the tree and freeing up its tangled, pot-bound roots. This will be a delicate task, but the tree will be much the better for it and its long-term survival all the greater.

The Constitution is far from simply what you see 'on its face' (as lawyers say), when you open its pages. It is a mixture of things that are stated, things that are implied, and things that depend upon unwritten rules or 'conventions', that is, on ways of doing things according to British parliamentary tradition. For those who do not understand British conventions, it must be utterly mystifying in places. As a guide to our political practices it is like using a nineteenth-century road map to find your way around your capital city.

In some cases, practices have changed over the years and this is the reason for the confusion, but a good number of these sections have never actually corresponded to practice.

In addition, a good number of practices have never actually been stated or even alluded to in the Constitution's words.

Consider what the Constitution says: That the Queen appoints the governor-general. That the governor-general makes the executive decisions and commands the naval and military forces, as her representative. That he appoints the members of the Ministry (or rather, 'the Federal Executive Council'); that these members 'hold office during his pleasure'.

Consider what it does not say: That Australia is a representative democracy, with a system of responsible government under the rule of law. That the government is formed by the party that commands the confidence of the House of Representatives. The leader of that party is the prime minister. That the members of the ministry are nominated by the government. That the governor-general acts upon the advice of his or her ministers.

The Constitution says, in fact, nothing at all about even the existence of the prime minister, although it has never seriously been imagined that we should do without one. It says nothing at all about how a government should be formed. If on election night, we turned to the Constitution for guidance, we would find none. The ABC's psephologist Antony Green would be a much better guide than the Constitution.

Is it likely that people would seriously think it more dangerous to write into the Constitution statements of our actual practices, than to leave in what is there at present, for example: 'The governor-general may appoint such times for holding the sessions of the parliament as he thinks fit'?

Some of the misleading provisions are unrelated to fundamental democratic principles but, taken with the other sources of obscurity, they create an archaic tangle, like morning glory vines wound tightly around the branches of the constitutional tree. The references to the Queen are in almost all cases misleading. The Queen simply does not exercise the powers or engage in the activities that the Constitution says she does. She is, the words tell us, part of the legislature; the executive power of the Commonwealth is vested in her; she is paid out of Australia's consolidated revenue so that she can pay a salary to the governor-general and to the ministers of state; she can disallow Australian laws, and so on. Queen Victoria did none of these things. Nor do 'Her Majesty's heirs and successors'. Even in the days of close imperial ties, it was the Australian or the British government that exercised such powers.

There are other archaisms we might like to tidy up while we are at it. All the Constitution's references to individuals—except the Queen—are to the masculine third person singular. Since the late nineteenth century, 'he embraces she' in statutory interpretation; that is, unless otherwise intended, where we read 'he', we are to understand 'he or she'. But why not now *say* 'he or she', and say what we mean?

I do not deny that our Constitution has worked and continues to work well. It is a restrained, 'minimalist' document and much of what it does say is still a functioning description of our practices. If you want to calculate a state's quota for seats in the House of Representatives or find the last date on which a federal election can be held in a particular year, the Constitution's your point of departure. The chapter on 'the Judicature' gets particularly good marks for accuracy, mainly because it was substantially based on the written United States constitution.

But even its staunchest defenders would have to admit that the Constitution often works well becaue what it says is ignored. The Queen does not appoint the governor-general. He does not determine the dates of parliamentary sessions 'as he thinks fit'. He does not choose government ministers nor, in normal circumstances, do they hold office during his pleasure.

The words of the Constitution are, of course, closely scrutinised by the High Court when a case arises, and the Court adapts and updates the meaning of words from time to time through its judgments. It has done so recently, for example, with the words 'citizen of a foreign power' (which are found in Section 44 of the Constitution), reading 'foreign' to include Britain and concluding thereby that a dual Australian–British national was ineligible to stand for parliament,[4] no doubt making the Constitution's framers turn in their graves. But most of the provisions concerning the parliament do not come before the court, except at times indirectly. They are normally 'interpreted' in practice, often by being ignored.

We may be quite comfortable in having to read between the lines of our Constitution, but we should not be complacent. The Australian convention that a Senate casual vacancy was filled with a nominee of the outgoing senator's party held good for the better part of three-quarters of a century. But the governments of New South Wales and Queensland departed from this convention in 1975; replacements were chosen by the respective premiers without consulting with the relevant Labor Party. The convention was deliberately breached, it appears, in order to change the distribution of power in the Senate. There was nothing in the Constitution to say this was not possible.

There is now. People agreed at the 1977 referendum that the old convention was important enough to be written down. They believed that there should be a statement in the Constitution requiring outgoing senators to be replaced by a nominee of their own party. I do not admire the cluttered and inelegant way in which the new Section 15 was drafted, but its example does serve to illustrate that problems can arise when fundamental practices are left to convention, and also that it *is* possible to get agreement on turning unwritten conventions into written instructions. Not all conventions can be easily converted into writing. Describing the governor-general's so-called 'reserve powers' is difficult and even possibly risky, although there is no reason to believe that the dangers are any greater in putting these powers into writing than leaving them unwritten. I happen to think that some sort of 'codification' of the reserve powers is both possible and desirable, not in order to describe our actual practices—since there are no regular practices—but rather to confine their use within our democratic system.

Whatever the eventuality or emergency the reserve powers should always be subject to the Constitution. The governor-general should only dismiss a government that has lost the confidence of the parliament and refuses to step down or that persists in other forms of unconstitutional behaviour; the governor-general should only exercise his or her powers to call an election, refuse to call an election or dissolve both Houses under the Constitution's double dissolution provisions (Section 57). This will all make much better sense once we have written into the Constitution the new, accurate descriptions of our fundamental democratic practices.

It may be difficult and will certainly take time to get

things right, but why should we prefer a constitution that says in places the opposite of what it means to a constitution that strives for accuracy?

Finally, looking into the mirror, we must attempt to describe what else we recognise. We need to ask ourselves: what was the original purpose of the Constitution? What was the basis of the 'federal compact' of 1901? Do we wish to renew it or alter some of the terms and conditions? Should we take it out for a thorough spring clean? Or should we simply assume that what people agreed upon one hundred years ago is the same as, and sufficient for, our needs at the Constitution's centenary?

I am—emphatically—not talking about dismantling the federal system and abolishing the states. For all the reasons Greg Craven gives in his Barton Lecture, we are stuck with the states. They serve us well, certainly better than a unitary system, and they correspond to subtle but definite cleavages. They promote participation and subsidiarity. I am talking rather about how well the Constitution still serves the 'indissoluble federal Commonwealth' for which it was designed.

The original federal compact consisted of an agreement on the part of the colonies to give up some of their self-government to the new Commonwealth parliament so they could enjoy the benefits of membership of an emerging nation-state. Many of these benefits were material. They included national defence, quarantine, co-ordinated postal services and lighthouse keeping, uniform immigration restrictions, access to a free national market and improved opportunities for attracting international investment.

But many were 'sentimental'—opportunities for international greatness, expanded cultural circles, an enhanced commitment to national welfare, and so on. The colonies gave up only those powers that were thought to be naturally or self-evidently 'national'. But they retained, or believed they retained, as much of their original autonomy as was compatible with membership of the Commonwealth.

This federal balance was clear in the distribution of powers between the levels of government. The problems it was designed to solve can be observed across a range of sections in the Constitution. Section 51 is a list of matters—such as defence, lighthouses and quarantine—in respect of which the Commonwealth parliament is empowered to make laws, 'for the peace, order and good government' of Australia as a whole. A few powers are exclusive to the Commonwealth. Most are concurrent: that is, able to be exercised by both levels of government so long as there is no inconsistency between them.

In 1901 many matters were left for the states: education, health, policing, road-building and so on. Each level of government was entitled to raise revenue appropriate to its powers and responsibilities. The colonies also gave a commitment not to exercise some of the powers they once held: for example, a famous section (Section 92) says: 'On the imposition of uniform duties of customs trade, commerce and intercourse among the states ... shall be absolutely free'.

It would have been clear one hundred years ago that this section meant that, once all the colonial protectionist tariffs had been removed, they should never be reimposed by the states. One hundred years later it is difficult for non-lawyers even to follow the words in this section, principally because we have forgotten the experience of being stopped at the customs houses on, for example, the Victorian borders, opening our luggage for inspection and paying protectionist tariffs on any dutiable items. The Constitution was intended as a happy, indeed blessed union, an indissoluble marriage of good sense and lasting affection. But is it exactly as we would want if we were going through the process in 2001? Are there things that we would now consider to be *national*, that are not currently able to be dealt with by the Commonwealth except in very roundabout way, through the Commonwealth's grant-giving power, or the application of international treaties, or through the states handing over certain powers to the Commonwealth?

Should there be, for example, a Commonwealth power over the incorporation of companies? Should the Commonwealth have greater control of environmental or natural resource regulation? Should the states regain the powers over universities that they lost when it was agreed in the 1960s that the Commonwealth would fund them?

Is the exclusive power of the Commonwealth to collect customs and excise duties appropriate now, given that the bulk of government revenue comes from income taxes and the states have effectively lost their power to collect taxes? We could multiply these questions. I do not necessarily support any of the proposals above, but give them simply as examples of what we would be likely to ask if the Federal Convention were meeting in 2001 instead of the 1890s and we were contemplating a federal compact.

This is not mere speculation. Questions along these lines were officially and fruitfully posed during the twentieth century and the Constitution has been altered a couple of times to meet the new understanding of what is properly 'national'. Powers over a range of social welfare provisions, including unemployment benefits and maternity allowances, were once thought to be essentially local matters, but were granted to the Commonwealth at a referendum in 1946. Special laws for the Aboriginal people were thought to be purely a state matter in 1901, not a national concern. In 1967, the provision preventing the Commonwealth from passing 'special laws' for the Aboriginal 'race' was deleted at a referendum.

Having missed out in 1901, should the Aboriginal people now be invited to the table where our imaginary new federal compact is being negotiated? Should the Commonwealth territories—units of the Federation allowed for in the Constitution, but not themselves parties to the compact (although their people voted in the referendums of 1898 and 1899)—now be represented?

Finally, it will follow naturally from most of these processes of constitutional pruning and composting that a republican constitution makes better sense than a monarchical one. Let us revisit our questions: is the Constitution intelligible to people today? Does it describe our actual democratic practices? Does it fit with our sense of the federal compact's purpose? If one applies these questions to the sections of the Constitution that refer to the Queen, the answer must surely be 'no' each time. I do not deny for one moment that the monarchy made sense to people in 1901, both as an institution and an object of affection. It was eminently sensible to federate 'under the Crown'. But, according to most available evidence, the monarchy is no longer intelligible to the majority of people in 2001. Almost all of the references to the Queen in the Constitution are now obsolete. The practices it ascribes to her would be abhorrent to our sense of democracy if they were accurate.

If, however, a thorough examination of the Constitution

concludes that the monarchy is still relevant, intelligible and accurately portrayed, republicans should pull their heads in. But I would be almost as astonished to find that this was the conclusion as I would to find Australians clinging to the statement that 'uniform duties of customs shall be imposed within two years after the establishment of the Commonwealth'.

In 1897 the Federal Convention received many petitions from individuals and groups, asking for particular things to be included in the Constitution. Some of these requests were met. For example, the reference to Almighty God, and a provision for individual states to control the sale or consumption of imported alcohol were both the subjects of many petitions and both ended up in the Constitution. A good number of other requests were rejected.

In our imaginary exercise of writing the Constitution in 2001, we will have to make similar decisions. A Bill of Rights and a statement of national 'values' will certainly be high on the list of requests, and many petitioners will support them. If I were a member of our imaginary Federal Convention, I would rise to my feet to argue the negative case. A Bill of Rights, if entrenched in the Constitution, attempts to set down as eternal and unchangeable what is, in fact, constantly in evolution. We often hear the framers of Australia's Constitution taken to task for failing to put rights into it. But what might they have included? No doubt many things we still regard as 'self-evident' these days. But, some things that many would now find questionable might well have been included; for example, the right to exploit and develop the country's natural resources and the right of children to be born in a legal marriage. And most people would now find repugnant what was the least controversial of all in 1897: the right to keep 'coloured' people out in order to protect the white nation.

The Constitution's framers would certainly not have included, indeed they would not even have identified, reproductive rights and sexual choice rights. Although they accepted that the Aborigines once owned the land, they would not have recognised their land rights. The fact that they did not entrench their own ideas of rights, based on their own values, is very much to their credit.

What—other than our confidence that we are right where others were wrong—makes us entitled to entrench our own view of rights? No doubt we live in more enlightened times. But, people believed they were enlightened in 1901. Who is to say that the future will not be even more enlightened and that those celebrating the bicentenary of Federation will not look back on us with the same scorn we reserve for our forebears? And how do we decide with certainty what those rights are to be, so that everyone sees them as 'self-evident'? Even very simple, apparently innocuous rights will raise much debate. For example, the right of all adult citizens to vote should be uncontroversial in a democracy. But not all adult citizens can, in fact, vote. Currently, prisoners serving terms of more than five years are not entitled to vote in Commonwealth elections. I happen to believe that, notwithstanding their convictions, they should retain the vote— indeed, that they probably have a greater need for representation in the parliaments than many outside the prisons. But many people would think otherwise.

Yet, if we included an unqualified statement in the Constitution that all adult citizens have the right to vote, the upshot may be that prisoners would have it too. That would be fine by me. However, I also believe that permanent residents should have the right to vote. They pay taxes as citizens do, and have no less need for representation. But a statement of citizens' rights to vote might rule out ever getting support for residents having the vote, short of through a referendum.

It is probably widely imagined by those who support an entrenched Bill of Rights that constitutional provisions work of their own accord, like putting out a note for the milkman at night and finding a pint on one's doorstep the following morning.[5] This is fanciful. Although the parliament is unlikely to push Acts through where they are blatantly unconstitutional, rights provisions—no matter how noble—will only come into play where there is a challenge.

Challenges only occur where an individual or a body with 'standing'—that is to say, where their interest in the issue at hand is recognised as valid by the court—brings an action. And they then can proceed only where the High Court gives leave for that action to be heard.

Who has the resources, ability, skills and funds to bring such actions? And what makes us so confident that the High Court will share our reading of rights anyway? If we marshal all the necessary resources and finally get before the bench, only to have our case dismissed, we will have no other place to turn to, and maybe even no cause for complaint. History shows that the majority of the 'rights' cases in the United States, and even those few cases we have experienced in Australia, tend to end with a victory for the larger, more powerful group.

On the other hand, if rights are not entrenched in the Constitution, they remain in the political arena. They can be legislated for, or recognised in legislation. Legislation can be amended, modified, updated or repealed when the necessity arises, without the need for a referendum. Those with individual claims can in certain cases take them to tribunals rather than the more expensive and limited courts. Those who want recognition for new 'rights' can agitate for political parties to adopt them. Rights notoriously 'collide'. Many claims over rights should never be simply decided in a win-or-lose form in any case, but require instead compromise, practical wisdom and recognition of the validity of many different perspectives.

There are many other practical problems. But the greatest danger lies where the attempt is made to tie rights and values together in a Constitution. If you begin to list Australian values, you run the risk that those who do not share them are left out of the picture, even regarded as 'un-Australian'. Certainly, values can sound aspirational, but often only to the generation that proposes them. Remember, people in 1901 found the Constitution inspirational. One hundred years later, we do not even remember the history of political innovation and experiment that inspired them, let alone recognise it in our Constitution, and we certainly do not find it adequate where we do.

We often tend to think that our personal values and interests should be the basis of public interests and policy. The problem is not just that it is very difficult—impossible—to have an ordered polity in which all interests are equally and adequately met. This is not just a technical problem of balancing one competing identity-based interest against another. Personal interests and the public good are qualitatively different things. The public is a different domain from the aggregation of personal interests or voices. The Constitution should serve the public good, not the separate parts.

It is all very well to propose such changes, but how will we ever achieve them? Most Australians know that the majority of referendums have failed; only eight out of a total of forty-four questions have succeeded. All sorts of hypotheses have been offered to explain this pattern. We cannot know for certain why referenda fail, but one thing is clear: people only support referenda when they can see some point in the proposed change. As time passes, and the Constitution makes less and less sense to people, it will become increasingly hard to see the point of piecemeal change. But piecemeal or partial change is not the only problem. The twentieth century saw many attempts at a wide-ranging, even total re-examination of the Constitution. Almost all of the commissions and committees and conventions set up over the years with such terms of reference produced detailed, distinguished reports and intelligent recommendations. But all in the end came to nothing.

Most recently, the 1998 Constitutional Convention concluded in an atmosphere of exhilaration, almost euphoria. Australians, it appeared, were on the verge of a breakthrough: a compromise over the way forward to a republic; an agreement over the contents of a new preamble. Three years later, with all that water under the bridge, who could imagine that the euphoria was ever justified? There is no realistic hope that a republican referendum might succeed in the current climate.

When we contemplate the difficulties Australians face in achieving even a relatively small—indeed, minimalist—change to our Constitution, the scale of writing an entire Constitution and of getting agreement on it, as happened in the 1890s, appears overwhelming. But, paradoxically, it may prove easier to begin again than to tinker around the edges.

What made the 1897 Federal Convention successful? To begin with, it was 80 per cent directly elected. The elected delegates had to see themselves differently from the way the parliamentary appointees of the first Convention saw themselves in 1891. They had to think about why the electors had put them there.

I am not suggesting that direct election worked because the delegates become the mouthpiece of those who elected them. This view would be very problematic, if only because of the number of different perspectives in the Australian population. But, being directly elected, the men in 1897 were obliged to look at the intentions of the federalist movement in a broad sense, not merely to look to party policy or personal views. They were working toward something new, not simply building upon the practices of previous governments. They were creating institutions that they knew they would, in many cases, not live to enjoy.

Of course, the 'Con Con'—the Constitutional Convention of 1998—was itself partly directly elected, and it did not succeed. Furthermore, it was directly elected in response to Australia's history, which suggests that parliaments and their nominees are not regarded as sufficient for the great purpose of changing constitutional direction. But the differences were crucial. For all the money and effort of election, the Con Con lasted for ten days only. Admittedly, its task was smaller than its nineteenth-century predecessor, but that Convention ran for a total of around sixteen weeks, spread out over a one-year period, with a recess for parliamentary and public scrutiny.

Not only did the elected delegates of 1998 have ten days alone to change the Constitution, but many of them could not even manage ten days. A significant number put proxies in their place for part of the time, and some of the prominent delegates attended for only two or three out of the total ten days. If legitimacy were to come from direct election, how could it be maintained in these circumstances? Above all the Con Con failed because it consisted of people on opposing sides of the question, not people who all wanted to work together on the task of constitutional change. These people were, of course, all entitled to be there. But the Con Con actually functioned as a ten-day public debate. It was a preliminary event—a conference—not a convention. It resembled the Federal Conference held in Melbourne in 1890, where appointed delegates debated the principle of Federation and concluded with a commitment to a future Convention.

The republican team won on points in 1998, but the work that should have been done at the Con Con—making decisions on all the matters that had to change if Australia were to become a republic—was left to a Senate committee and to the Commonwealth parliamentary draftsmen. What should have been a considerable advantage—direct election—was not sufficient. In one respect, however, the Con Con was a genuine improvement on most of the other twentieth-century attempts to review the Constitution, and closer to its 1897 counterpart. It was multi-partisan. It was not associated with one political party, or split along party lines. This undoubtedly remains a necessary precondition for the success of any attempt, large or small, to change our constitution.

There is another—perhaps the fundamental—requirement for a successful attempt to rethink the Constitution. An outlook that is genuinely broad, generous, constructive and 'national' is crucial. Not every single member of the

1897 Federal Convention had such an outlook, but the majority of them made a genuine attempt.

This type of outlook is, alas, becoming rarer and rarer in Australia, on every side of politics. In the 1890s the problem was 'provincialism', but it was at least a manageable target. These days, however, we increasingly regard the political as a sphere in which our own individual identities, built around gender, sexuality, race, ethnicity, region, youth, and so on, must be directly represented and the interests that are assumed to arise from our identity must be met. We conclude that there are specific rights attached to these identities. We have lost sight of the fact that our values and those of the nation are not and cannot be the same thing.

The attempt to write a new preamble in 1999 involved a scramble to list every major identity group in case someone was upset at being left out. And it represented a deeply disturbing attempt to define the nation's values. We were asked to commit ourselves to certain values and to be proud of certain things, *as Australians*. This had the effect in me at least of drawing out those other 'Australian' characteristics of stubbornness, perversity and the conviction that, however much I might agree, I wanted the right to change my mind. Fortunately, the majority of other Australians in 1999 thought something similar.

The experience of 1999 is perhaps a small, but optimistic sign that, if seen through a non-partisan, 'national' frame of mind, a new broader-reaching constitutional convention may have some hope of success.

So what am I saying? That the Constitution needs changing, that it needs a total—not a piecemeal—rethink, and that this will be difficult, but not impossible to achieve. But is my conclusion no more than that we need a practical, 'plain-words' Constitution, with the dead wood cut out, with our democratic institutions and practices stated simply in an intelligible way, and with the 'national' sorted out from the regional, and powers distributed appropriately? This would certainly be an improvement on a constitution that is both uninspiring *and* unintelligible. But for many there will be something inherently unsatisfying, even empty, in a purely functional constitution.

A constitution (as Edmund Barton said) is not a dog licence. It is not a simple ordinance that states bluntly what has to be done and whether some one can or cannot do it. At the same time it is not a desideratum. It cannot be a wish-list or a prayer or an alternative national anthem. It has to function, not just by having a practical connection with our political and legal system, not just because it has to guide our political institutions. It also has to serve a community of diverse and evolving values. It will simply not work if it tries to meet everyone's values—because values, like rights, 'collide', because they are not fixed and eternal anyway, and because the resources that support them are finite.

Nor is the Constitution a party platform. Many want to write into the Constitution what are effectively policies. The unsuccessful 1999 preamble, for example, told us to be 'mindful of our responsibilities to protect our unique natural environment'. Many might agree, but others may consider it equally desirable to exploit and make use of our natural environment. It told us that we value 'equality of opportunity'. Some would consider equality of opportunity to be insufficient and economic equality to be the goal. These are all legitimate alternatives that should be debated in the political arena, not excluded because they are left out while alternative views are entrenched in the Constitution.

The good news is that there will always be mystery in a Constitution because it has to meet circumstances that can never be fully known in advance. Its symbolic power will never be reducible to plain words. But we should not seek inspiration for its own sake. What will inspire some, or even many, will certainly not inspire all. We should stop imagining that other countries have intrinsically more inspiring constitutions and that we are somehow being short-changed. We should emulate the restraint of our Constitution's framers. We should avoid a 'feel-good' constitution, if only because it will soon look out of date and we will find ourselves wearing constitutional flares when straight-legs are in.

Is it really impossible for us to be inspired by a democratic, simple and flexible Constitution, one that makes sense and can be read by, even taught to non-specialists?

When we look in the constitutional mirror we do not yet find the frame empty and the reflection blank. But, unless we engage with the Constitution in a manner unparalleled since its creation, unless we remove and renovate much of its content and reaffirm what we want to retain, we will find in the future that this is the result. We shall have a constitutional identity only in our past, and our dreams of alternatives will become surreal. The Justices on the High Court will be the nation's psychoanalysts. The silver will have come away completely from the back of the mirror. Re-silvering is an expensive and difficult business. Few tradesmen with this skill are still around. Let's not wait until they have all gone.

ENDNOTES

1. *Official Record of the Debates of the Australasian Federal Convention*, Melbourne 1898; Legal Books, Sydney, vol. v, p. 2516.
2. ibid., p. 2502.
3. ibid., p. 1732.
4. *Sue v. Hill* (1999) 163 ALR 648.
5. I am indebted for this metaphor to Dr John Williams from the School of Law at the University of Adelaide.

AFTERWORDS

GEOFFREY BOLTON

Edmund Barton revisited

After spending several years in writing a biography, one is apt to become either deeply disenchanted with the subject or inescapably prejudiced in his or her favour. In either case, it is probably unwise to revisit a career shortly after publishing the biography. What is there fresh to say? Nevertheless, having listened with relish and occasional outbursts of disagreement to the Barton Lectures, I found it easy to succumb when Helen Irving invited me to attempt 'a short essay on Barton and his significance to Australia in the centenary year'. Apart from the fortuitous distinction of coming first among our twenty-five prime ministers, what is there about the career of Sir Edmund Barton that matters a damn to the Australian citizens of 2001?

Barton was born near Sydney in January 1849 and died in the Blue Mountains west of Sydney in January 1920. He was a member of the first generation of non-Aboriginal Australian-born adults and his life spanned the period from the eve of the discovery of gold to the end of World War I. Until he was forty he was an easygoing lawyer and colonial politician, who did well during a four-year term as Speaker of the New South Wales Legislative Assembly, but was otherwise no more distinguished than a hundred of his Australian contemporaries. During his last sixteen years, he was an adequate but hardly outstanding High Court judge. Barton's imprint on Australian history rests on fourteen years of his early middle age, from the Lithgow speech of November 1889 which ranked him beside Sir Henry Parkes as an advocate of Federation and ensured that the movement would be non-partisan, to his resignation as federal prime minister in September 1903.

During his lifetime some accused Barton of idleness, and since his death he has been dogged by the 'Tosspot Toby' label invented by the malevolent editor of *Truth* John Norton, but undeniably during those fourteen years he worked hard and achieved much. He came to the fore during the first National Australasian Convention of March–April 1891. Although he was not fond enough of committee work to win Alfred Deakin's approval, he was by far the best prepared member of the New South Wales delegation, at two critical moments intervening with constructive speeches that eased debate around points that might have split the delegates. As a last-minute subsitute for Tasmania's Andrew Inglis Clark among the drafting party on the Queensland government ship the *Lucinda*, which hammered out the text of the Constitution over Easter 1891, he more than earned his place. He left the Convention marked as one of the rising stars of the Federation movement.

But Federation was not yet sure. Perhaps influenced by

the precedent of Canadian confederation in the 1860s, Parkes imagined that the parliaments and senior politicians of the federating colonies could do all that was necessary to bring the new Commonwealth into being. He failed to push the legislation through a New South Wales Legislative Assembly in which the new Labor Party held the balance of power, and shortly afterwards lost office. Lacking a lead from New South Wales, the other colonies held back. Except for Western Australia, they were all more or less engulfed in the worst economic depression for fifty years. Federation seemed a lesser priority.

As attorney-general in the Dibbs ministry that replaced Parkes' in New South Wales, Barton held a weak hand. His premier, George Dibbs, was no believer in Federation and in 1894 would propose a centralised model, with New South Wales and Victoria unifying into one state and the rest of Australia following when it was ready. In later years the political scientist and historian L.F. Crisp, and other supporters of strong central government, have lamented that the Dibbs model was not followed, but it strains the imagination to think of Queensland and Western Australia joining a union where all power was located in the southeast. Barton never lost his conviction that the federal way was the route for Australia to travel.

Barton also realised that the Federation movement must enlist grassroots support. The most promising ground for mobilising such support was the Riverina district, separated by tariffs from what many considered their natural markets in Victoria. During the winter and spring of 1892 a number of communities in the Riverina began to form pro-Federation pressure groups. Once aware of these developments, Barton travelled to Albury and Corowa in December 1892 and there launched the first Federation League. They were not quite the first pro-Federation lobbies, since in Victoria the Australian Natives' Association was already vocal in the cause, but Barton was the first prominent politician to identify with an organisation specifically dedicated to promote Federation.

By July 1893 a national Federation League was established in Sydney—though to Barton's embarrassment the opening meeting was almost taken over by republicans—and at the end of that month the Federation Leagues convened the Corowa conference, at which Barton was not present, though he endorsed its recommendations. At Corowa the plan emerged for a second Convention with delegates elected by the voters of each colony. This Convention should produce a constitution for ratification at plebiscites in each colony. If a majority of voters in each of the Australian colonies said 'Yes', the Commonwealth of Australia would become the first nation created at the ballot-box.

Between 1894 and 1897 Barton was out of parliament and sorely beset by debts. He continued to campaign for Federation, often to small and apathetic audiences, and in later years was apt to claim credit for carrying on the crusade as a private citizen rather than a politician. It was nevertheless that most professional of politicians, his old friend and rival Free Trader George Reid, who persuaded his fellow premiers to accept the Corowa formula and to support a second Convention, beginning in March 1897.

But when New South Wales chose its ten delegates, it was Barton who topped the poll as 'Mr Federation' with a chagrined Reid in second place. Reid nevertheless backed Barton to lead the business of the 1897 Convention and

Barton rose to the occasion. In three sessions—Adelaide in March 1897, Sydney in September and Melbourne in January–March 1898—he steered the fifty delegates to an agreed draft constitution. His authority was never seriously challenged after his success at Adelaide in beating back an attempt by the smaller colonies to undo the 1891 compromise defining the powers of the Senate. If some of the decisions taken in the later stages of the Melbourne session smacked of weariness and expediency rather than statesmanlike forethought, this was hardly the fault of Barton, whom his secretary Robert Garran remembered as labouring all night over successive drafts of the Constitution.

For some such as Reid, however, Barton's quest for workable compromises resulted in some dubious decisions for New South Wales. When the draft Constitution was submitted to the voters Reid's attitude of qualified and tepid support saddled him with the name of 'Yes-No' Reid, but appealed to democrats fearful of the supposedly conservative influence of the smaller colonies. Barton's wholehearted advocacy of Federation won a narrow majority at the June 1898 referendum in New South Wales, but it was not enough to meet the quota required for a valid 'Yes' vote. It was only after Reid wrung a few more concessions from his fellow premiers that Barton and Reid campaigned together at a second referendum in June 1899 to secure New South Wales as a member of the Commonwealth. South Australia, Tasmania and Victoria had already voted 'Yes'. Queensland followed in September 1899. In New South Wales and Queensland Barton was considered the leading speaker on the 'Yes' side. His normally overelaborate oratory was refined by repetition and sincere conviction into a compelling message that won through to the voters.

Early in 1900 Barton went to London as leader of the delegation monitoring the progress through the British parliament of the Bill creating the Australian Commonwealth. The delegation encountered strong resistance from the British authorities against Section 74 of the Bill limiting appeals from the Australian High Court to the Judicial Committee of the Privy Council, and were white-anted by legal and business interests in Australia who wanted overseas appeals to continue. Powerfully supported by Deakin and South Australia's Charles Kingston, Barton eventually won a compromise and in the process made a good impression on the officials of Downing Street.

These officials, like most Australians, expected that the incoming governor-general, Lord Hopetoun, would invite Barton to serve as first prime minister. On his arrival in December 1900, however, Hopetoun gave the commission to form the first ministry to Sir William Lyne as premier of the senior colony, New South Wales. Deakin and George Turner of Victoria, Frederick Holder of South Australia and others refused to serve under Lyne, who was not an enthusiast for Federation. Lyne ultimately advised Hopetoun to send for Barton, who formed a ministry in time for the inaugural celebrations of 1 January 1901.

Quite apart from his symbolic status as leader of the Federation movement, Barton suited the strong-minded ex-premiers who formed the bulk of his first Cabinet. He had not previously been their colleague and equal, and he was an excellent chairman. In order to avoid problems of status he arranged that the Cabinet should meet at a round table.

Barton lasted as prime minister until September 1903. The main achievements of his ministry were the White Australia

Policy, the enfranchisement of women, the renegotiation of a naval agreement with Britain, the establishment of a national protective tariff, the takeover of Papua as an Australian responsibility and the creation of the High Court.

In a parliament in which no party held a majority in either House, the Barton government's most significant achievement was probably to achieve political stability while the infrastructure of Australia's public service and defence were set in place. Despite a spell of depression for several months and his absence for several more months at a conference of British Empire prime ministers, Barton's performance as prime minister was more creative than has often been recognised.

Barton went to the new High Court in September 1903, yielding the position of Chief Justice to Sir Samuel Griffith whom he acknowledged (rightly) as the abler and more incisive jurist. For much of his sixteen years on the Bench he seemed Griffith's loyal echo, though in old age he asserted a greater independence, and was sorely disappointed when, after Griffith's resignation in 1919, he was not appointed to succeed him, despite the unanimous support of his colleagues. Hig poor health told against him and in January 1920 he died while on holiday at the Hydro-Majestic Hotel at Medlow Bath in the Blue Mountains. He was the last survivor of the effective first Federal Cabinet.

Barton was not as able an orator as either Deakin or Reid. He lacked some of the political canniness that served Reid well in negotiating the terms of Federation with his fellow premiers, and he does not match Deakin as a creative user of power seeking to steer Australia in new directions. His comparative lack of creativity, in fact, fed his greatest strength: his ability as a broker of stable consensus. Himself somewhat conservative, he was still open to new concepts such as women's suffrage or federal industrial arbitration, and his readiness to change his mind gracefully rather than push an intransigent agenda accounted for a good deal of his political success. As a judge, removed from the need to accomodate a variety of interests and anxious for the preservation of the hard-won federal agreement he returned to a greater conservatism.

Barton's career may seem remote from the concerns of the early twenty-first century. Several of its major landmarks have now lost validity. Multicultural Australia cannot applaud the White Australia Policy. Barton's capacity to see himself simultaneously a proudly Australian citizen and a loyal adherent of the British Empire no longer resonates for most Australians, though an alternative sense of national identity is still in the evolutionary process. Tariff protection has lost its appeal in an era of globalisation. Even Federation itself is often criticised as saddling Australia with too many politicians and too confused an allocation of government responsibilities.

Nevertheless, several aspects of Barton's life deserve consideration. First, his education. Before qualifying as a lawyer, Barton took his Master of Arts degree at the University of Sydney, majoring in the Greek and Roman classics under an internationally distinguished professor, Charles Badham. Badham's strength lay in his editing of the texts of Socrates, Plato and Aristotle, with meticulous attention to the precise definition of the meanings of the original Greek words. This skill is of the same order as the skill required in legal draftsmanship or judicial interpretation, forming a sound foundation for Barton's work as a constitutionalist.

Socrates, Plato and Aristotle, citizens of Athens in the

fifth and fourth centuries BC, were taught in universities in the ninteenth and early twentieth centuries because they discussed many of the fundamental questions of political philosophy with the clarity and excitement of explorers opening up a subject for the first time. Aristotle in particular, with his doctrine of the golden mean—the middle way between extremes—would have appealed to Barton's temperament. Like his predecessors, Aristotle taught that politics should be conducted ethically. The desirable qualities in a political leader he summed up in his portrait of the 'magnanimous man':

The magnanimous man, since he deserves most, must be good, in the highest degree ... Therefore it is truly hard to be magnanimous; for it is impossible without nobility and goodness of character ... It is the mark of the magnanimous man to ask for nothing or scarcely anything, but to give help readily, and to be dignified towards people who enjoy a high position but unassuming to those of the middle class ... a lofty bearing over the former is no mark of ill-breeding, but among humble people it is as vulgar as a display of strength against the weak ... He is one who will possess beautiful and profitless things rather than profitable and useful ones ... Further, a slow step is thought proper to the magnanimous man, a deep voice, and a level utterance ...[1]

It would be absurd to suggest that Aristotle's magnanimous man served as an exact role model for the young Barton, who loved cricket and fishing, still less to the politician making his way in a New South Wales legislature dubbed 'the bear-garden of Macquarie Street', but some of Barton's characteristics recall Aristotle. Bertrand

Russell observed:

> A modern democracy—unlike those of antiquity—confers great power upon certain chosen individuals, Presidents or Prime Ministers, and must expect of them kinds of merit which are not expected of the ordinary citizen . . . In a democracy a President is not expected to be quite like Aristotle's magnanimous man, but still he is expected to be rather different from the average citizen, and to have certain merits connected with his station. These peculiar merits would perhaps not be considered 'ethical', but that is because we use this adjective in a narrower sense than that in which it is used by Aristotle.[2]

Sensitive on points of personal honour, Barton placed great stress on behaving well and presenting well as a public figure. He was noted for his courtesy towards supporters and opponents alike, and in his pursuit of the Federation ideal he was notoriously indifferent to his own income. On the whole, it seems that the Australian public of one hundred years ago found those qualities admirable.

The Greek and Roman classics have dwindled in university curricula, but we have not found a satisfactory substitute for the educational background of aspiring politicians. As one who taught at the University of Western Australia during the undergraduate careers of several who in later life were prominently involved in the 'WA Inc' scandals of the late 1980s and early 1990s, I strongly doubt the adequacy of current tertiary education as a grounding for public life. It remains puzzling that recent federal governments, although they show great enthusiasm for imposing bureaucratic quality control procedures on universities, have shown no interest in developing indices of quality control for parliamentarians.

In earlier generations it was usual for a parliamentary candidate to experience a significant period in the wider workplace before entering politics, and this experience often shaped their personal values. Ben Chifley, the engine driver with an ingrained sense of working-class solidarity and belief in social justice, Robert Menzies the barrister, product of a legal culture that stressed Burkean precedent and the importance of good order, each brought to political leadership an ethical dimension (though this was quite compatible with political guile and the enjoyment of office).

In the current federal parliament there are more tertiary graduates than ever before, and according to Dr Geoffrey Hawker's calculations, more members— perhaps 30 per cent of the whole—whose entire working life has been spent in politics, having served as research assistants, union officials or party functionaries before securing endorsement for a seat, preferably at an early age.[3] It is far from clear that their education has included any political philosophy, or indeed any instruction about the practical workings of Australian political institutions in a comparative perspective.

Barton, with his classical education that at first sight might seem so removed from the practicalities of Australian politics, in fact came to parliament better prepared than many modern politicians. Barton's political education could not be called a case of theory without democratic practice. Like every other politician of his generation he took part in election campaigns that involved a large and unpredictable amount of street theatre. Campaigners in shire halls or on hotel balconies addressed crowds of hundreds, or sometimes thousands of uninhibited male voters, whose rough wit and awkward questions needed skill and personality to handle. When things got rough missiles such as old eggs, bags of flour and rotten fruit might be pelted at a speaker. Today's politician, confronting even the most probing of interviewers in the insulated comfort of the television studio, is a good deal further removed from the reality of the voters in their sitting-rooms watching him or her on 'the box', and they see a less spontaneous performance.

Barton, Reid, Deakin and their contemporaries staked the success of the Federation movement on their capacity to persuade the voters of each of the six colonies of Australia to return a 'Yes' majority. This was accomplished in just over two years of intensive campaigning between 1898 and 1900. Even when account is taken of the groundwork previously done by the Federation League and the Australian Natives' Association in south-eastern Australia, this is an impressive achievement, especially considerating how few referendums during the hundred years of the Australian Commonwealth have won the same level of support. Part of this success was no doubt due, as John Hirst argues,[4] to the existence of a widespread sense of national sentiment among the Australian public, but part must have been due to the skill of Barton and his colleagures in appealing to that public and convincing them that the federal Constitution as drafted would befit that sense of national sentiment.

It is worth stressing this point. Labor and radical writers and speakers at the time of Federation complained that the Constitution was undemocratic because the smaller states would outvote Victoria and New South Wales in the Senate. Behind this fear lay a characteristically smug assumption that Victoria and New South Wales were less conservative and more politically enlightened than Western Australia or Tasmania. This proved at best debatable, but some subsequent historians have continued to complain that the advocates of Federation rushed their formula on to the voters instead of taking time to perfect a better model. They share none of Deakin's sense of miracle that any form of Federation was found acceptable, and none of Barton's pragmatic expectation that, once created, the Australian Constitution was capable of further improvement as time suggested the necessity to a majority of voters in a majority of the states.

These lessons were forgotten by the protagonists of republicanism in 1999 and their opponents. Hypnotised by the advent of the Sydney Olympic Games and the new millennium, they sought to force a decision without sufficiently preparing or educating a public who, on every indication, were willing to accept an Australian republic. Their failure may be a sign that the gap between politicians and the general public has widened during the last hundred years. Not that Barton's methods offer any solace to advocates of participatory democracy or citizen-initiated referendums. The work of framing the Contitution was done by professional politicians and lawyers, and when the public had an opportunity of choosing delegates to the 1897–98 Convention they voted for professional politicians, many of them lawyers (except for J.T. Walker of New South Wales, a businessman who had never been in politics but who made amends later by becoming a member of the first Senate). The voters must have thought that these delegates could be trusted to produce a constitution with which they could live comfortably, and their choice was vindicated by the majority of 'Yes' votes which followed.

Doubts are rife about the ability of today's federal politicians to command similar trust, but the causes of these doubts defy easy analysis. Some commentators point to the boorish behaviour of MPs in times of excitement, but today's House of Representatives at its most turbulent is a kindergarten compared to the Legislative Assembly in which Barton presided over the 'wild men of Sydney' in the 1880s.

Others blame the stultifying effect of an over-disciplined two-party system. It is true that on the rare occasions when debate in the House of Representatives is permitted free of party allegiances, the quality of the dialogue improves noticeably. There has seldom been a higher level of conscientious and thoughtful debate than the speeches made on the Lusher amendment of 1979 seeking to restrict government funding for abortions, and this was an issue on which tempers might have been expected to run high.

Opinions about the durability of the two-party system differ among veteran politicians. Some believe that it will still be the dominant paradigm a hundred years from now, though others foresee a continuing rise among minor parties and independents, eventually forcing a resort to the coalition-mongering normal among many European and East Asian parliaments. Already the necessity of cutting deals with the Democrats and the minor parties in the Senate has required federal governments to recover a dexterity in negotiation hardly needed since the Fusion of 1909 ushered in an effective two-party system. Barton would have recognised the qualities of flexible compromise needed in such negotiations, though they may not appeal to those who prefer patterns of command drawn from the business world.

Nevertheless the culture of the two-party system dominates discourse in the House of Representatives, an adversarial culture often compared to the rivalry between two sporting teams. It may be no coincidence that the increasing professionalisation of sport during the last twenty or thirty years—also its commercialisation—has been matched by an increasing public perception that politics in Canberra is played as a boys' game, with the emphasis on winning at all costs. Quality of debate is sacrificed to crushing the other side. A team leader with the rottweiler instincts and biased historical understanding of Paul Keating is perceived as a masterly parliamentarian.

It is not necessary that the politicans of the twenty-first century should try to resurrect the political culture of Barton and Deakin, but it is desirable that they should come to their job properly educated. It is not necessary to replicate the pomp and ceremony of the opening of parliament in 1901, but it might be useful to restore the sense that the honour of representing the people of Australia in parliament is a position of dignity, and that the behaviour of Australian politicians should include more than a touch of Aristotlean magnanimity.

The present generation of Australian male politicians might have been too strongly influenced by the concept of parliament as theatre of adversarial sport to restore that touch of magnanimity. In ways that neither Aristotle nor the politicians of Barton's generation could easily have imagined, we may need to rely on the women in politics to raise standards of parliamentary conduct. The example of such MPs as Neville Bonner, Aden Ridgeway and Carol Martin suggests that these standards would be reinforced by our Aboriginal representatives.

ENDNOTES

1. Aristotle, *Ethics* (1123b–1125a), quoted in Bertrand Rusell, *History of Western Philosophy*, George Allen & Unwin, London, 1946, pp. 197–8.
2. ibid., p. 200.
3. Geoffrey Hawker, reported in *Weekend Australian*, 5–6 May 2001.
4. John Hirst, *The Sentimental Nation: The Making of the Australian Commonwealth*, Oxford University Press, Melbourne, 2000.

ELAINE THOMPSON

The Australian Commonwealth: One hundred years of continuity and change

In the background of all the Barton Lectures are three questions: What sort of democracy is Australia? Who are we as Australians? and: What matters to us?

These questions highlight both our unity and our diversity. Across the past hundred years they have involved changing ideas about equality, rights, representativeness, and the role and nature of our constitutionally based political institutional arrangements. The ideas have also been dramatically affected by (and in turn have directly influenced) our changing place in the world; our changing economic structure; our changing demography and our changing social makeup.

What sort of democracy? Equality and representativeness

The history of Australia from the mid nineteenth to the end of the twentieth century can be viewed as the history of a society that defined democracy in terms of equality and had a particular view of the role of government with respect to equality. What changed across the century was what was meant by equality, particularly with respect to class, gender, ethnicity, race and region (and, though rarely discussed, religion). The Australian 'way of doing politics' has explored equality less from its philosophical meanings and more from its legal and institutional aspects and in very straightforward and identifiable terms of equality of outcomes. It has not been much concerned with theories; it has been greatly concerned with what happens.

What also changed towards the end of the century were views about the role of government. At Federation, Australian democracy centred on attempts by government to guarantee equality to white males through, among other things, the White Australia immigration policy and tariff walls protecting their relatively high wages and conditions. Arrangements were also in place guaranteeing what, for the time, was wide access to the franchise.

Since Federation, equality developed, first to bring

women into the voting and political arrangements, then progressively extended to people of various ethnicities, and finally to the Aboriginal people. Legal, institutional equality now formally exists for all. Australian democracy has become much more representative and it has embedded legal equality.

Equality of outcomes in what actually happens is a much more varied story, with indigenous people remaining the single most disadvantaged group. While most of the twentieth century told a class-based story of closing the gap of differences in income and wealth, the end of the century saw that gap open again and pointed to economic arrangements that are likely to embed class-based inequality, and within that class-based inequality questions of gender, ethnicity and region.

While the Labor Party has existed for the entire period since Federation and remains strongly linked to the trade union movement, the overall positions of trade unionism is much weaker than it was by the middle of the twentieth century, and the hard-fought protections gained with Federation in terms of industrial rights are under challenge at the beginning of the twenty-first century.

For most of the twentieth century, non-urban regions enjoyed special protections, including special tax arrangements and at state level a highly inegalitarian arrangement of electoral districts to give rural Australia much greater parliamentary representation than its numbers warranted.

Since the 1970s those voting arrangements have disappeared and since the 1980s many of the special protections of the country have been replaced by further hardships. The end of the twentieth century has seen, through the rise of the politics of reaction—especially in the form of the One Nation party—a rethinking and a return to a more protectionist attitude to rural Australia.

What sort of democracy?
Institutional structures

Most federation fathers would not be surprised by the government's domination of parliament, for that was already happening; and strong parties emerged relatively quickly and dominated (and continue to dominate) politics. What has changed is the role of the media. Newspapers were prolific, widely read and important at the start of the twentieth century, and they are still important because politicians take them extremely seriously. They remain the most important agenda-setting source of ideas for other news media. However, television, talk-back radio and today the Internet are also important, because of the way they present the world, Australian society and Australian politics.

Voters have also changed. From around 1910 to around 1970 Australian voters were extremely stable and loyal. By the end of the 1960s great changes began, not least because many women stopped automatically following the voting preference of their husbands or fathers and emerged by the 1980s as independent. Today one-quarter of Australians vote away from the major parties in their first preference choice in the House of Representatives and are even more volatile in their vote for the Senate, where they regularly ensure that minor parties hold the balance of power. Moreover, by the 1990s the number of swinging voters increased, so that seats once considered safe (blue-ribbon Liberal or heartland Labor) are safe no longer, with swings of 10 to 20 per cent.

Despite these changes, the Constitution has remained extremely important. Because of the Constitution, the central government was unable to nationalise the banks in the 1940s; because of the Constitution, workers in the same company can be covered by entirely different awards affecting their wages and conditions of work; because of the Constitution, the central government cannot set uniform safety standards or standards for environmental protection. And the corporation's power (Section 51 (xx)) has meant that there is no direct national economic management because the centre cannot control prices, monopolies or many financial institutions and arrangements.

These strictures and limitations created by the Constitution have remained powerful forces across the century. On the other hand, were the federation fathers to look at the system today most would probably be surprised to see how big and dominant the central government now is, and how the states have lost so many powers. Decisions of the High Court and decisions by the states themselves with respect to taxing powers have progressively altered the constitutional balance in fundamental ways: the centre now virtually controls all major revenue raising.

Furthermore, as Australia grew, the emerging needs and aspirations of its people were met by the Commonwealth rather than the states. The centre has been able to initiate programs in almost every important area of policy, if it believes it is in its electoral interests to do so.

In some ways expansive government was to be expected: the optimism at the beginning of the twentieth century that Australia could achieve social and economic equality inevitably involved governments that wanted to do things. Moreover, governments always played a large role in Australia. As early as the 1870s public investment represented 30 to 40 per cent of total investment, and by 1900 public authorites employed about 10 per cent of the national workforce, something like twice the percentage employed by the United States government.

For most of the twentieth century government not only carried out the various normal functions such as foreign affairs, trade, education, health and welfare, but also ran airlines, universities, banks, scientific research, television and radio stations, gas, coal, electricity and oil, brickworks and aluminium companies. There were government-organised marketing boards for all important primary products—eggs, milk, meat, wheat, dairy products and wool. There were advisory bodies such as the Grants Commission, adjudicatory review bodies such as the Conciliation and Arbitration Commission and regulatory bodies such as the Australian Broadcasting Control Board.

In what can rightly be described as a revolution in the role of government over the last twenty years, government has shed many of these functions, either wholly or particularly, either through outright sales, corporatisation or contracting out.

All these changes took place within a world context of change with the opening up of competition, instant communications, instant movement of capital, a move to a service economy and an internationalisation of labour.

The role of government has been reduced. The private sector is the preferred sector *prima facie*.

WHO ARE WE AS AUSTRALIANS?

Changing notions of equality also profoundly affected the way we think about ourselves. In fits and starts, Australia emerged in the last third of the twentieth century not only as a democracy committed to equality but as a more liberal society. That development involved recognising differences—a dramatic move away from the single-white-race, single-culture intolerance that marked the first fifty years since Federation. Tolerance of the views of others and demcratic mechanisms to resolve the differences now partly define what an Australian is—at least to most Australians. Australians' enthusiasm for reconciliation with the Aboriginal people is perhaps the clearest indicator of the change.

WHO ARE WE? FROM SUBJECTS TO CITIZENS

Of all the great changes over the hundred years since Federation, none is more profound than our relationship with the rest of the world. Indeed, some Barton lecturers argued that Federation did not involve the making of a sovereign nation because Australia was unequivocally a part of the great British Empire and its people subjects, not citizens. The British monarchy was relevant, and few Australians were interested in republican ideas. Australia saw itself as dependent on Britain and believed it would be defended by that great power. Yet today the Empire is scarcely remembered, let alone understood.

The great change was largely a result of World War II when Britain could not defend Australia and the country found itself defended by the United States navy (as well as its own efforts). Following World War II the British legacy continued, in the sense that Australia's tradition of great power dependency continued and Australia sought guarantees of protection from the emerging great power, the United States. That pattern has continued.

Australia's reorientation away from Britain not only involved the United States, but from the 1950s an engagement with Asia. Reorientation was also signalled in the development of multiculturalism as a defining cultural policy of Australia, replacing a cultural policy defined with reference to the English-speaking world, and in the vigorous debate over whether Australia should break its last ties with Britain and become a republic.

Who are we? Social and demographic change

Accompanying the changes in attitudes on gender, race and ethnicity are vast changes in the demographics and social conditions of Australians and what work means in Australia. Until the 1950s the vast majority of workers were male and unskilled. Until the late 1970s unions were very powerful and workers normally remained in a particular area of work, with employment virtually taken for granted. As Rick Farley and Belinda Probert eloquently demonstrate in their Barton Lectures, that has all gone. Employment and promotion on the basis of merit have replaced the seventy-year-old tradition of promotion by seniority, and continuous employment in a single field of occupation, whether for unskilled or for professional people, no longer exists.

Another important change has been the entry of large numbers of women, including married women, into the total labour force. Around 40 per cent of the workforce are women, two-thirds of them married. There has also been a major change in favour of part-time and casual work rather than full-time work. Over one-quarter of the labour force was born outside Australia, and more than 1.2 million do not have English as their first language. Language and gender appear as the prime determinants of income levels.

While the majority of Australians still live, as they did one hundred years ago, in Western 'nuclear families', there have been great changes in family structures. In 1973, 33 per cent of Australian women were married by the age of twenty. In 1993 the figure was around 5 per cent. The number of those who remarry is also increasing: in 1973 about 90 per cent of Australian marriages were first marriages; in 1993 the figure was around 60 per cent. The number of children per family has declined. Six per cent of all couples are not formally married, but in common law relationships. In more than half of all families with dependent children both parents work, a dramatic shift away from the Australian lifestyle when the norm was for the husband to be the sole breadwinner.

Like many Western societies, Australia has a large

proportion of people who live alone. Around 20 per cent of people live by themselves. Since the mid 1970s there has been a 55 per cent increase in the numbers living alone—the largest growth of any group by household size. At the turn of the twentieth century the concern was with unmarried, lonely men; at the turn of the twenty-first, most people living alone are women.

There has been a vast change in access to, and use of, education. For most of Australia's history, education was undervalued. As recently as 1981 only 35 per cent of children completed twelve years of schooling. By 2001 it was over 70 per cent. The impact of this change in education has been great. With the leap in the number completing the maximum twelve years of school, the demand for tertiary education exceeded the number of places and put heavy demands on universities and technical institutes.

What matters to us? Tolerance and liberal ideas

There have been major extensions of tolerance, both towards people from different backgrounds and with respect to issues such as religion, prostitution, abortion and censorship. Since the 1960s by and large there has been, and continues to be, a commitment to a more liberal, tolerant society, backed if necessary by government legislation or government guidelines in areas such as film censorship to ensure a more liberal approach. There has also been a liberal move away from government's 'right to conceal', to deprive citizens of access to information about policy-making and about themselves. The development of consumer rights, and of the 'new administrative law' of the 1970s signalled a change towards the 'public's right to know' with the introduction of freedom of information legislation, the development of the ombudsman's office and of administrative appeals tribunals to which an individual could appeal against a decision on the basis of whether it was 'fair and reasonable' rather than according to the old standard of legality. Citizens could now gain access to their own tax files, immigration, social security and credit records, and correct these where necessary. In addition in the 1990s, government and private sector organisations developed 'charters of duties and responsibilities' and 'customers' rights'. While many of these are more public relations exercises than commitments, they nonetheless signal a changed set of expectations.

What matters to us? What are our rights?

Linked to the rise of a more liberal society has been the idea of rights. As Helen Irving and Mary Kalantzis noted in their Barton Lectures, the Constitution did not and does not even mention voting as a right, and indeed makes no mention of Australian citizens and any of their rights—no mention of freedom of speech nor freedom of association. To be fair the Constitution specified that the Houses of Parliament were to be directly elected, deadlocks between the two Houses would be solved by going to the people, and plural voting was banned. British common law rights were assumed to exist in Australia and to protect its citizens, despite those protections not applying to the indigenous people and often, when it suited state governments, not applying at all. During the 1960s and 1970s the Queensland and Western Australian governments in particular suspended the right to demonstrate and the right of association whenever they felt these rights might embarrass them.

However, the idea of individual rights was clearly articulated through the 'new politics' of the 1960s and 1970s: gay rights, women's rights, children's rights, students' rights, indigenous peoples' rights, ethnic rights and the protection of the environment in particular. The High Court reinforced the importance of other rights, especially Aboriginal rights, but also in some areas, the rights to free speech and rights against discrimination more generally.

By the late 1980s, as Donald Horne pointed out in his lecture, there were some challenges to the idea of these rights, as representing narrow 'special' minority interests; however despite the challenges, the assertion of rights is part of politics today.

There is nonetheless still some debate, as is obvious if you compare Helen Irving's views with those of Mary Kalantzis, about the best ways of protecting these rights. What is no longer really debated is the fact that while the Australian system is very strong on the rule of law, rights protection is deficient. There is debate over whether or not Australia should adopt a Bill of Rights, whether or not such a Bill should be entrenched in the Constitution, and what rights should be protected.

What Matters to Us? From 'National Development' to 'the Economy'

Donald Horne has traced the revolution from the 'national faith of development' that emphasised great projects such as the Snowy Mountains Scheme and the development of BHP and the Holden car to today's post-industrial economy in which more people work in service industries than anywhere else. Much discussion on inequality in Australia, and on the response of both government and the changing social structures, revolves around the stresses and strains that revolution brought with it.

Some things have not changed. Exports remain important, and Australia is almost unique amongst Western advanced economies in its heavy dependence on its primary sector for its exports. But even in the primary export sector, what we produce has changed: we no longer ride on the sheep's back. From 1850 to 1950 wool's share in Australia's total export income was around 40 per cent; by the 1980s it was around 10 per cent. Half our export income today comes from minerals, fuels and metals.

Whom we trade with has also changed. Japan, Europe generally, and the United States have grown dramatically in importance while Britain has declined. The developing countries, especially those of South East Asia, have also become important. In the 1950s these countries bought less than 20 per cent of Australia's exports, but now account for more than one-third. Japan and South East Asia account for 40 per cent of Australia's total trade.

In line with the internationalisation of economics and the deregulation of industry, Australia over recent years has changed its policies dramatically in the manufacturing area. This area was the most protected, having grown up behind high tariff barriers as well as within a heavily regulated financial environment with controls on financial markets, exchange controls and controls over foreign investment. These financial regulations have either been removed or lessened significantly, as have the tariff barriers.

As in other post-industrial developed countries, many Australian manufacturing companies have been forced to close, including manufacturing of white goods, clothing, shoes and motor vehicles, with many people put out of work as a result. On the other hand, Australians now have available to them a much more diverse range of products at prices much more competitive by world standards.

In 2001 Australia's single most important economic sector consists of services accounting for about three-quarters of total output. This sector includes industries such as wholesale and retail trade, finance, property, food, business services, transport, communication, tourism, education, health and construction. Over the last twenty-five years world tourism has increased fourfold.

What matters to us? Policy changes

At Federation the optimistic view of material well-being meant a concern with social justice. That concern was embedded with the establishment of the Commonwealth Arbitration Court to set minimum wages and conditions. That Court continues to protect workers at the bottom of the heap. Since the 1980s however, wages and conditions have increasingly been negotiated at a company or individual basis through enterprise agreements, dramatically reducing the role of government and unions in the negotiations.

Beginning in the 1930s and expanding for the rest of the twentieth century, social justice also involved the development of pensions and other government-run benefits, including unemployment benefits, compulsory superannuation, and medical and hospital benefits. As these benefits developed, they were seen as a citizen's and/or worker's 'right'. The 'right' to these benefits fell under review by the end of the twentieth century. Immigrants in their first two years after arrival are not eligible to receive most of them, and most benefits are now subject to a policy of mutual obligation whereby, for example, the unemployed are expected to carry out volunteer or other work. The role of government as guarantor of social justice has changed with respect to these schemes of income support.

Nonetheless government has continued to develop policies concerned with social justice, most dramatically with respect to the indigenous people, women and immigrants from non-English-speaking backgrounds. Commencing in the 1980s, governments have put in place powerful anti-discrimination legislation, anti-racial vilification legislation and equal employment opportunity legislation.

At the start of the twenty-first century, governments

are now responding to new issues to do with pollution—especially salination and global warming—as well as entirely new areas of policy: *in vitro* fertilisation, genetically modified food, Internet gambling and pornography, and electronic fraud. Of equal importance are new policies in old areas now involved in massive technological developments, for example medicine and education. Finally, governments and citizens are faced with a plethora of problems flowing from the changed nature of work and society: drugs, organised crime, youth suicide, the impact of deregulation, permanent unemployment, the needs for retraining and multiskilling, and the problems of an ageing Australia.

Perhaps if some of the federation fathers were to come back they would be duly impressed by all the technological wonders, startled at the nature of multicultural Australia, disappointed that governments had not been able to make poverty disappear, depressed by so many new problems—but bemused that so many old institutions have changed so little, including the way politics works, the parties and the Constitution. They would feel at home in Canberra.

The Contributors

PROFESSOR DONALD HORNE has written more than twenty books (including *The Lucky Country*) and contributed to journals and newspapers in Australia, Britain, Europe and the United States. He was twice editor of *The Bulletin*, edited the *Observer* and *Quadrant* and was contributing editor to *Newsweek International*. He became a professor at the University of New South Wales and Chancellor of the University of Canberra. He has played an active part in a number of cultural organisations, including the Australia Council, which he chaired for six years, and has served on a number of bodies concerned with constitutional reform.

PROFESSOR BELINDA PROBERT is Head of the School of Social Science and Planning at RMIT University. For the past decade her research and writing have focused on the changing nature of work and employment and new patterns of advantage and disadvantage. She has written on the impact of globalisation, technological change in the workforce and the increasing tensions between work and life, and has carried out research for a number of trade unions and community organisations on work and family issues.

MR RICK FARLEY is Managing Director of the Farley Consulting Group, which specialises in land use agreements. He is also chairman of the NSW Resources and Conservation Assessment Council, an ambassador for reconciliation and co-chair of the NSW State Reconciliation Committee. A key figure in the passage of the Native Title Act in 1993, he worked for rural organisations for 20 years, was Executive Director of the National Farmers' Federation and the Cattlemen's Union of Australia and now provides advice to a range of development companies and Aboriginal communities throughout Australia.

DR ELAINE THOMPSON is an associate professor in the School of Politics and International Relations at the University of New South Wales, where she teaches public policy and Australian and United States politics. She has been Visiting Research Professor and Senior Fulbright Fellow, Center for Presidential and Congressional Studies at the American University, Fulbright Fellow with the Department of Political Science, Pennsylvania State University and International Visitor at the United States State Department.

PROFESSOR LOIS BRYSON is one of the founders of academic sociology in Australia, with a career spanning four decades. Her books include with Faith Thompson *An Australian Newtown* (1972), with Ian Winter *Social Change, Suburban Lives* (1998) and *Women and Survival* (1994). She remains an active contributor to government policy and to community organisations, particularly those focused on women and the welfare state. She is a Chief Investigator of the Women's Health Australia project, a large multidisciplinary study planned to follow, over twenty years, the health and well-being of more than 42,000 women.

DR JOHN HIRST is Reader in History at La Trobe University. He is the chair of the Commonwealth Government's Civics Education Group which is overseeing the preparation of materials for the 'Discovering Democracy' program in schools. He was founding Convenor of the Australian Republican Movement in Victoria and a member of the Prime Minister's Republic Advisory Committee (1993). His history of the Federation movement, *The Sentimental Nation*, was published by Oxford University Press in December 2000.

PROFESSOR MARY KALANTZIS is the daughter of Greek immigrants, a professor of education, a university executive, a public commentator and a prolific writer on culture, education, history and politics. Her work has focused on settler, immigrant and indigenous diversity in Australia's history, and how these differences in history and life experience intersect with each other. Her writing, in collaboration will Bill Cope, includes *A Place in the Sun: Re-Creating the Australian Way of Life* (HarperCollins, 2000), *Multiliteracies: Literacy Learning and the Design of Social Futures* (Routledge, 2000) and *Productive Diversity* (Pluto Press, 1997).

MS LYDIA MILLER, a Guguelandji woman, originally qualified and practised as a nurse before moving into the area of indigenous arts, first as an administrator and then as performer, producer and director. Her performance as an actor is widely recognised. She is a member of the Cultural Network of the Australian National Commission for UNESCO, and a Council member of the Australian Film and Television School. She is currently completing her studies in Arts/Law at the University of Sydney.

Professor Greg Craven is a constitutional lawyer and historian, and has published widely in these fields. He is Provost and Foundation Dean of Law at the University of Notre Dame Australia in Fremantle. Prior to this he was a Reader in Law at the University of Melbourne, and he served for three years as Crown Counsel for Victoria. He was an appointed delegate to the 1998 Constitutional Convention and a member of the Yes Committee for the 1999 republican referendum.

Dr Helen Irving is a Senior Lecturer in the Faculty of Law at the University of Sydney. She is a member of the Education, History and Civics Advisory Committee of the NSW Centenary of Federation Committee, a former member of the Council of the Constitutional Centenary Foundation and member of the Advisory Council of the National Archives of Australia. She is the author of *To Constitute a Nation* (Cambridge University Press, 1997 and 1999), editor of *A Woman's Constitution?* (Hale & Iremonger, 1996) and *The Centenary Companion to Australian Federation* (Cambridge University Press 1999) and co-editor of *No Ordinary Act: Essays on Federation and the Constitution by J.A. La Nauze* (Melbourne University Press, 2001). With Donald Horne, she is co-author of the booklet '2001: Why Are We Celebrating?' (NSW Centenary of Federation Committee, 2000).